MEDIUM ÆVUM MONOGRAPHS
EDITORIAL COMMITTEE

K.P. CLARKE, G. DAVIES, A.J. LAPPIN,
S. MOSSMAN, P. RUSSELL, C. SAUNDERS

MEDIUM ÆVUM MONOGRAPHS
XLV

# LIBER DE DUOBUS MONACHIS VEL DIALOGUS PERSECUTORIS ET ZELATORIS RELIGIOSORUM

## A CRITICAL EDITION OF A FOURTEENTH-CENTURY LATIN DIALOGUE POEM

Edited by
Laurence Eldredge

The Society for the Study of Medieval Languages and Literature
OXFORD · MMXXIII

THE SOCIETY FOR THE STUDY OF MEDIEVAL LANGUAGES AND LITERATURE

https://aevum.space/monographs

© Laurence Eldredge, 2023

British Library Cataloguing in Publication Data
A catalogue record for this book is available from the British Library

ISBN-13:

978-1-911694-18-2 (pb)
978-1-911694-19-9 (hb)
978-1-911694-20-5 (pdf)

*In memoriam*:
A.P. "Phonse" Campbell (1912-1983)
editor, *The Tiberius Psalter* (1974)
æghwæs untæle ealde wisan

# CONTENTS

Acknowledgements ................................................................ ix
Abbreviations ........................................................................ xi
Introduction ........................................................................ xv
   (a)  The Manuscripts ........................................... xviii
   (b)  The Artistry of the Poem ............................. xxvii
   (c)  Influences ...................................................... xxx
   (d)  Monastic Life ............................................... xxxii
   (d)  The Text of the Edition ............................... xxxiii
*Liber de duobus monachis* ................................................. 1
Bibliography ....................................................................... 101

# ACKNOWLEDGEMENTS

This edition had its beginnings at Columbia University in a 1960s' doctoral dissertation, supervised by Professor W.T.H. Jackson, under whose guidance I learned that the Middle Ages were not dark and consisted of much more than Chaucer. I also owe thanks to others, both friends and faculty, at Columbia in the late 50s/early 60s and at the University of Ottawa in the 70s/80s. I am also indebted to the trenchant comments of A. George Rigg, of the University of Toronto, and anonymous readers at University of Toronto Press, where I submitted an earlier edition based on Co alone. More recently I owe large debts to Christine Glaßner of Melk Stiftesbibliothek, especially for calling the Graz manuscript to my attention; to Juliana Dresvina; to Sinéad Hofmann for mathematical wizardry; to Peter Murray Jones for guidance to medieval art; to the late Nigel Palmer (1946-2022) for his exacting and helpful encouragement; to Lesley Smith for her very skilled assistance through the publication process; to Leen Van Broeck; to Frank Vanlangenhove of Ghent University Library; to Iolanda Ventura; to Carolinne White for her critical eye on my Latin and enviable computer skills; and to Stephen Pink and Anthony Lappin for seeing this edition through the mill. And not least I am extremely grateful to an anonymous reader for Medium Ævum Monographs, and even where I have not followed their suggestions I have done considerable rethinking. It is a special pleasure to acknowledge their drawing to my attention the Ottobonian manuscript at the Vatican. I should like to thank the several libraries which have generously allowed me to quote from the manuscripts in their possession: Universiteitsbibliotheek Gent, Biblioteca Apostolica Vaticana, the Rare Book and Manuscript Library of Columbia University, Melk Stiftesbibliothek, and Graz Universitätsbibliothek. Finally, I owe an unpayable debt to my wife, Karin, whose constant support and able assistance cannot be summed up in a single adjective. The inevitable errors that remain are all my own doing.

L.E.

# ABBREVIATIONS

(Biblical abbreviations according to ed. Rome Tournay Paris, 1956)

| | |
|---|---|
| AASS | J. Bolandus, G. Henschenius, and J. Carnaudet, eds., *Acta Sanctorum*, 85 vols. (Paris, 1643-1931) |
| Act | Actus apostolorum |
| Apoc | Apocalypsis ... Joannis |
| Ca. | Circa instans, in "Incipit liber de simplici medicina secundum instans platerarium dicitur circa instans," *Practica Jo. Serapionis dicta breviarium. Liber Serapionis de simlplici medicina. Liber de simplici medicina dictus circa instans Practica Platearii* (n.p., n.d. but clearly incunable). Also Hans Wölfel, *Das Arzneidrogenbuch Circa instans* ... (Berlin, 1939). |
| Cant | Canticum canticorum |
| CCSL | Corpus Christianorum Series Latina |
| CL | Classical Latin |
| Co | New York City, Columbia University, MS. X878C86/P, ff. 1r-22v. |
| I, II Cor | Epistola ad Corinthios I and II |
| Dan | Prophetia Danielis |
| DTC | *Dictionnaire de théologie catholique* |
| Deut | Liber Deuteronomii |
| Ec | Ecclesiastes |
| Eccli | Ecclesiasticus |
| Ex | Exodus |
| Ez | Prophetia Ezechielis |
| FL | L. Hervieux, *Les fabulistes latins*, 5 vols. (Paris, 1893-99) |
| Gal | Epistola ... ad Galatas |

xii                  Abbreviations

| | |
|---|---|
| Gen | Genesis |
| **Gh** | Ghent, University of Ghent Library, MS. 2178, ff. 155r-190r. |
| Gr | Graz, Universitätsbibliothek MS. 1359, ff. 2r-8r, 37r-40v. |
| Greg | Gregorii magni, *Dialogi libri IV*, ed. Umberto Moricca (Rome, 1924) |
| Hebr | Epistola ... ad Hebraeos |
| Iac | Epistola ... Iacobi |
| Ier | Prophetia Ierimiae |
| Ioan | Evangelium ... Ioannem |
| Iob | Liber Iob |
| Ion | Liber Ionas |
| Ios | Liber Iosue |
| Iud | Liber Iudicum |
| LDM | Liber de duobus monachis |
| LSSM | Jakob Werner, *Lateinischer Sprichwörter und Sinnsprüche des Mittelalters* (Heidelberg, 1912) |
| Luc | Evangelium ... Lucum |
| I, II Mach | Liber I, II Machabaeorum |
| Marc | Evangelium ... Marcum |
| Matth | Evangelium ... Matthaeum |
| **Me** | Melk, Stiftsbibliothek Melk, MS. 800, ff. 55r-63r |
| Num | Numeri |
| I, II Petr | Epistola Petri I and II |
| **Ot** | Vatican, Biblioteca Apostolica Vaticana, MS Ott. lat. 522, ff. 134r-141v |
| PL | J.-P. Migne, *Patrologiae Cursus Completus, series latina*, 221 vols. (Paris, 1878-90) |
| Prov | Liber proverbiorum |

| | |
|---|---|
| Ps | Liber psalmorum |
| I, II, III, IV Reg | Liber regum I, II, III, IV |
| Reg mon | St Benedict, *Regula monasteriorum*, ed. Benno Linderbauer, Floralegium patristicum, fasc. 17 (Bonn, 1928) |
| Sap | Liber sapientiae |
| Tob | Liber Tobiae |
| Walther | Hans Walther, *Proverbia sententiaeque latinitatis medii aevi*, Carmina Medii Aevi Posterioris Latina, 5 vols. (Göttingen, 1963-67) |

# INTRODUCTION

It is pretty well agreed that Medieval Latin literature reached its height in the long twelfth century, where skilled poets developed their own mastery of the language, the possible styles, an independent relation to the Roman classics. Poems like Walter of Châtillon's *Alexandreis*[1] and Joseph of Exeter's *Ylias*[2] demonstrate an easy mastery of metrical hexameters and a distinctively medieval attitude toward the material, while *Ysengrimus*[3] (possibly by Nivardus of Ghent) turns great skill with elegaic distichs toward a satiric dismantling of monastic corruption and greed. At the same time many poets, mostly anonymous, capitalised on the newly developed accented verse rhythm and produced lyrical masterpieces, mostly anonymous, mostly satirical.[4]

The *Liber de duobus monachis* provides a late example of a well-established genre known as Dialogue[5], which begins around the time of Sulpicius Severus[6] (d. ca. 420) and includes such works as the

---

[1] Galteri de Castellione *Alexandreis*, ed. Marvin L. Colker (Padua, 1978).
[2] Joseph Iscanus: *Werke und Briefe*, ed. Ludwig Gompf (Leiden, 1970).
[3] *Ysengrimus*, ed. Ernst Voigt (Halle, 1884) and more recently Jill Mann (Cambridge, MA, 2013) with English translation.
[4] It would be impossible to list here a full bibliography of medieval Latin poetry, but for a start see F.J.E. Raby, *A History of Christian Latin Poetry*, 2nd ed (1953) and *A History of Secular Latin Poetry*, 2 vols., 2nd ed. (1957), and A. G. Rigg, *A History of Anglo-Latin Literature 1066-1422* (Cambridge, 1992).
[5] See the extensive study of C. Cardelle de Hartmann, *Lateinische Dialoge 1200-1400: literaturhistorische Studie und Repertorium*, Mittellateinische Studien und Texte 37 (Leiden, Boston, 2007), who does not record the LDM. Earlier, Hans Walther, *Das Streitgedicht in der lateinischen Literatur des Mittelalters* (Munich, 1920) identified a subset of dialogues, debate poems, and dealt briefly with the Melk manuscript of LDM on pp. 167-68.
[6] *Sulpicii Severi Libri qui supersunt*, ed. Carolus Halm CSEL (Vienna, 1866) and Richard J. Goodrich, *Sulpicius Severus: the Complete Works. Introduction, Translation, and Notes* (New York, 2015).

*Dialogus miraculorum* of Caesarius of Heisterbach[7] (ca. 1180-1240) and the *Dialogus* of William of Ockham[8] (d. ca. 1347), to mention only these examples. Cardelle de Hartmann's thorough study concludes that there is no standard form, no typical dialogue, and very few dialogues in verse;[9] though they often consist of a novice, a tyro, posing brief questions to a novice master or similar authority figure, and the master replying at greater length. Usually he expounds orthodox doctrine, either directly or by means of stories, and the genre is unabashedly didactic. The LDM, however, differs from the tradition in that the novice, known as the Persecutor, is not really a novice but a monk of some experience in monastic life,[10] most of it not very pleasant. Rather than ask advice he criticises and vituperates and complains about various aspects of life in a monastery. The first third of the poem is devoted to this type of generality where the Persecutor remarks on such vices as fraud, hypocrisy, simony, jealousy, malice, envy, pride, and so on. But at line 589 the Zelator, his interlocutor, asks for specifics:

> Iam tibi nec fides nec ero bene credulus ultra
> Exemplum nisi des quo mala facta probes.

And the Persecutor responds with specific accounts of three abbots, under whom he served and incubated his critical catalogue of monastic life. When we first meet him, he has decided to give up being a monk for something unspecified, but by the end of the poem the quiet persuasion of his older companion has made him change his mind. And that sort of counsel puts the poem firmly in the Dialogue tradition.

---

[7] Caesarii Heisterbacensis, *Dialogus miraculorum*, ed. Joseph Strange (Cologne, 1851) and Caesarius von Heisterbach, *Dialogus Miraculorum über die Wunder*, eds. N. Nösges and H. Schneider, Fontes Christiani (Turnhout, 2009), with German translation.

[8] William of Ockham, *Dialogus*, eds. J. Kilcullen et al. (London, 1995-2015).

[9] Cardelle-de-Hartmann, p. 263.

[10] At l. 10 the poet refers to the Persecutor as 'leuem puerum' (slender youth), but his experiences suggest that he is no novice.

As far as I know, LDM is the only account of medieval monastic life told by those who experienced it.[11] Eadmer's *Life of St Anselm*[12] tells the story of an inspirational abbot whose monks probably thrived under his leadership, but the LDM allows us a glimpse of monastic life as it was lived by those who were neither abbots nor priors but ordinary garden-variety monks in monasteries led by abbots rather less adroit than Anselm. Moreover, there seems little hint that the dialogue it presents is connected with one of the great monastic reform movements, like the Cluniac reforms that started in the tenth century and reverberated for some centuries thereafter. Here the focus is not on monasteries themselves as part of an interconnected web of similar institutions, but rather the personal account of one monk who met with nothing but trouble in his monastic life and a second probably older monk who slowly, gradually convinces him of the value of cloistered life. In contrast to the majority of dialogues,[13] the last word goes to the Persecutor, who declares himself reformed and ready to return to the cloister.

Technically the poem is written in elegiac distichs—that is, a metric hexameter followed by a metric pentameter. Of course our poet is not so skilled a metricist as his classical forebears, nor even as good as the twelfth-century poets, Walter of Châtillon and Joseph of

---

[11] The recent *Cambridge History of Medieval Monasticism in the Latin West*, eds. Alison J. Beach and Isabelle Cochelin, 2 vols. (Cambridge, 2020) mentions monastic living conditions only in passing. For a possible reason for this lack of information, see Wojtek Jezierski, "*Verba volant, scripta manent*: Limits of Speech, Power of Silence and Logic of Practice in some Monastic Conflicts of the High Middle Ages," in Steven Vanderputten, ed., *Understanding Monastic Practices of Oral Communication*, Utrecht Studies in Medieval Literacy (Turnhout, 2011), pp. 23-48, outlines the monastic practice of not recording in writing the details of conflicts and turmoil, in order to protect the privacy of the monastery from the secular world.

[12] Eadmer, *The Life of St Anselm Archbishop of Canterbury*, ed. and trans. Richard Southern (Oxford, 1962).

[13] Cardelle-de-Hartmann, pp. 289-703, presents detailed accounts of 79 Latin dialogues in the majority of which the last word goes to the authority figure.

Exeter.[14] But he is every bit as good a metricist as Nivardus of Ghent, the twelfth-century author of *Ysengrimus*,[15] despite the frequency of diaeresis, where the end of a metric foot and the end of a word coincide. But there is almost no use of leonine hexameters, where the syllable before the caesura and the final syllable rhyme. There is a good deal of end-rhyme although only on a single unaccented syllable,[16] and I confess that my ear is not keen enough to find that feature offensive.

## THE MANUSCRIPTS

There are five known manuscripts of the poem. I list them here with their sigla to the left:

**Gh** Ghent, Universiteitsbibliotheek Gent, MS 2178, item 10, ff. 155r-190r, incipit: Claustralis vite quondam sanctissimus ordo. Modern foliation, inferior parchment (some holes, some damaged leaves), 165 x 120 mm, writing area 100 x 65 mm, attractive mise-en-page with wide margins, apparently good condition, though seen only in a pdf copy. Collation: i-iii⁸, iv⁶, catch-words. Title in lower margin f. 155r, 20 lines to the page, each line of verse occupying a line of writing, pentameter not indented, dry point pricking evident throughout, horizontal and vertical lines faint but visible. Catalogued in Albert Derolez, Hendrik de Foort, and Frank Vanlangenhove, *Medieval Manuscripts: Ghent University Library* (Ghent, 2017), p. 256, who place the origin of the manuscript somewhere in southern Belgium. The codex, assembled and bound in the nineteenth century, is a collection of unrelated miscellaneous texts in theology, canon law, medicine, sermons (in French), ars dictaminis, etc. The text of LDM can be

---

[14] Walter and Joseph as in notes 1 and 2, above. See also the opinion of A.G. Rigg, (cited in note 4), p. 102.
[15] Cited in note 3, above, with detailed discussion of the prosody on pp. xxxi-xxxvii.
[16] Just out of curiosity I counted some end rhymes: LDM—52, Ysengrimus—23 in the first 1412 lines, Aeneid VI—24.

dated to the 1370-80s.[17] There are two hands[18], the principal hand and the hand of the marginal commentator. The principal hand is a tidy, legible book hand, with a single-compartment a; b, h, l normally unlooped; two-stroke c and t easily confused with one another and often with r; d has left leaning ascender; g horned on the upper right, descender loops left and often includes a hairline back to the upper lobe; m, n, and u carefully distinguished from each other; both straight and round s; two-stroke straight r; punctus elevatus at the end of the hexameter for the first folio and a half, thereafter sporadic. Second hand cursive, round d with a looped ascender; l, h occasionally looped; m, n, and u distinct; two-stroke c and t; straight s often descends below the baseline; abbreviation for cum/con/com two-stroke with descender hooked to right. Provenance: Liège, Benedictine Abbey of St. James. Gift of Prof. Jean-Henri Bormans, ca. 1836-40.

**Ot** Vatican City, Biblioteca Apostolica Vaticana, MS Ott. lat. 522, ff. 134r-141v, incipit: Claustralis vite quondam sanctissimus ordo. Parchment, 13th-14th century, good condition, 158 x 110 mm, writing area 128 x 98 mm, untitled, contemporary foliation, no catch-words and thus collation impossible to determine. **Ot** is a codex largely dedicated to Franciscan matters, described by Livarius Oliger, O.F.M., 'Bonagratia de Bergamo et eius tractatus

---

[17] See François Masai and Martin Wittke, *Manuscrits datés conservés en Belgique*, vol. I: 819-1400 (Brussels, 1968), plate 63, dated 1377, from Brussels, Bibliothèque Royale, MS II 2297, f. 178v, where the hand is similar to but tidier than Gh, with the same g, though a two-compartment a, a round r. Plate 66(a), dated 1383, from Brussels, BR, MS 10893-94, f. 62v, a hand slacker than plate 63 but closer to Gh with the same g and same a. Plate 67(a), also dated 1383, from the same MS, f. 13v, with a more heavily abbreviated text and tidier than **Gh**. The second hand, that of the marginal commentator, is similar to Plate 203(b), dated 1388, from Brussels, BR, MS 2695-719, f. 105v, a more cursive hand with a round d with a looped ascender.

[18] For paleographical vocabulary I rely on Albert Derolez, *The Paleography of Gothic Manuscript Books from the Twelfth to the Early Sixteenth Century* (Cambridge, 2002), especially the Glossary, pp. xx-xxi.

de Christi et apostolorum paupertate,' *Archivium Franciscanum Historicum*, 22 (1929), 292-335. The manuscript probably dates from after 1340, the date of Fr Bonagratia's death. **Ot** consists of two separate manuscripts; ff. 1-141 forms part I and ff. 142-321 part II. Part I, containing LDM, also contains miscellaneous texts, mostly Franciscan, some theological (St Jerome's letter to Heliodorus, St Austustine's treatise on charity, two commentaries on Franciscan rule by Angelo Clareno and St Bonaventura, Bonagratia de Bergamo on the poverty of Christ and the Apostles [edited in this article from this MS and from Paris, BN lat 4046 by Fr Oliger, pp. 323-335], fragments of Peter John Olivi and John Pecham) and others secular (Aldobrandus de Tuscanella on three-stranded rope, where he notes similarities with the Trinity, notes on grammar, etc). The second manuscript in **Ot** also presents Franciscan texts but is unrelated to the first manuscript. Part I of **Ot** is written in a variety of hands, a different hand for each of the thirteen items, the whole described by Fr Oliger, who is generous with his comments on the contents of the manuscript. The text of LDM appears cramped with narrow margins and tightly spaced lines but is in fact carefully copied and, apart from a few water stains, quite legible. Moreover, its text corresponds almost exactly with that of **Gh**. On ff. 134r-135v the text presents 2 lines of verse in a single line of writing, but from 136r-141v the poem is written in two columns and each line of verse is given a single written line. The hand in which LDM is written is not particularly attractive, and the narrow margins give the mise-en-page a cramped and unappealing appearance. I have been unable to identify a similar hand in any of the catalogues of dated and datable manuscripts, but the only examples that come close seem to have been written in the Low Countries at a date before the probable date of **Ot**. I found only three examples of hands that shared some of the letter forms: a two compartment a, a two stroke c, single stroke d with the ascender leaning left, long f and s which do not descend below the baseline, a horned g whose tail curves left with a hairline connecting it to the lobe, an h whose

Introduction xxi

right descender curves left, m n u not distinguished from one another.[19] I would not argue that these hands share enough characteristics with LDM to be even related, but perhaps they are earlier examples of a hand that eventually evolved into the hand in LDM.

Co   New York City, Columbia University, Rare Book and Manuscript Library, MS X878C86.P, ff. 1-23, incipit: Credite quicquid erit ego uester homerus ubique. Paper, 216 x 152 mm, writing area 152 x 95 mm (30 lines to the leaf), good condition, unfoliated and unpaginated, untitled, purchased from the antiquarian book dealer William Salloch in 1957, collation: i⁷ [ff. 1-14] and ii⁶ [ff. 15-26, originally an 8, for knife cuts are still evident on ff. 14 and 26, indicating the removal of leaves after the poem was copied], bound in modern paper wrappers with what appear to be dealer's marks at the top: the number 49 in red crayon (also at the foot of f. 1r) and two notes in pencil: RiVI/07 and bo. Lines and margins lightly drawn in ink, dry-point pricking evident in the first gathering, largely trimmed from the second, 30 lines to the page, a single line of verse occupies a single line on the page, with the pentameter line indented. There are two poems in Co, the poem that figures in this edition and on ff. 23r-23v, a florilegium of snippets in rhythmic hexameters from other Medieval Latin poems.[20] Both poems are written in the same hand, a mid-fifteenth-century book hand with some cursive features, probably

---

[19] See Masai and Wittig, *Manuscrits datés*, Plates 116 and 121, both dated 1332. Also see Charles Samaran and Robert Marichal, *Catalogue des manuscrits en écriture latine*, II—Planches (Paris, 1962), Planche XLA, dated 1305 and probably written in the Low Countries.

[20] Hans Walther, *Initia carminum ac versuum medii aevi posterioris latinorum* (Göttingen, 1959), ll. 1-33 = Walther 13457, l. 24 = W 17011, ll. 35-6 = W 3072, ll. 37-51 = W 902a, ll. 52-3 = W 1884a, ll. 54-55 = W 13454.

from the Upper Rhine area.[21] The hand typically shows a single compartment a; a two-stroke c and t that can be confused; a horned g with open lower loop—it resembles a modern handwritten y with a horizontal stroke across the two minims; an h whose right descender curves left; i normally dotted; b h l normally looped (double l usually not looped); both straight and round s; u and n carefully distinguished. Dating of **Co** is confirmed by the two watermarks in the two gatherings, which also suggest a mid-fifteenth century date and a scriptorium somewhere in the Upper Rhine area.[22] The provenance of **Co** remains elusive. A letter to me from William Salloch, 4 August 1961, states in part: "... I have been digging in our records, trying to find a clue to the provenience [sic] of the manuscript, but I am

---

[21] Cf. Matthias Scarpetti et al., *Katalog der Handschriften der Schweiz in lateinischer Schrift vom Anfang des Mittelalters bis 1550*, 3 vols. (Dietikon-Zürich, 1977-1991). See vol. I, p. 98, Abb. 241, dated 1436, Basel, Univ.-Bibl., A X 138, f. 127r; p. 164, Abb. 407, dated 1460, Basel, Univ.-Bibl., AN V 12, f. 17r; p. 200, Abb. 499, dated 1468, Basel, Univ.-Bibl., A XI 37, f. 97ra; p. 209, Abb. 521, dated 1471, Basel, Univ.-Bibl., A XI 44, f. 84rb. Vol II, p. 236, Abb. 564, dated 1494, Bern, Burgerbibl., MS 801, f. 2v. Winfried Hagenmeier, *Die datierten Handschriften der Universitätsbibliothek und anderer öffentlichen Sammlungen in Freiburg im Breisgau und Umgebung* (Stuttgart, 1989), p. 111, Univ.-Bibl., Hs 19, f. 118v, dated 1480 at Memmingen. H. Spilling (based on earlier work by W. Irtenkauf), *Die datierten Handschriften der Württembergischen Landesbibliothek Stuttgart*, Teil 1: *die datierten Handschriften der ehemaligen Hofbibliothek Stuttgart* (Stuttgart, 1991), pl. 142, MS XIV 20.1, f. 272v, dated 1453 (written by Jacob Pernhart de Ratisbona [Regensburg], very similar though not identical to Co).

[22] See C.M. Briquet, *Les filigranes*, 2nd ed. (Leipzig, 1923), no. 11803 (a mountain surmounted by a tall cross), dated at Innsbruck 1468. This seems to be an exact replica of the watermark on the paper in the first gathering, unrecorded in Gerhard Piccard, Findbuch XI *Wasserzeichen Kreuz*. The second gathering has a squat tower as a watermark, not identical to any in Briquet, but similar to several others in Piccard, *Der Turm* (Stuttgart, 1970), Findbuch III, Abteilung ii, 324-53. Further examples at www.piccard-online.de/suche.php?sprache=de (accessed 5/3/21) also fail to reveal an exact copy, but all these examples dating from 1448 to 1465 were produced in the Milan area and distributed for the most part northwards in Switzerland and Germany.

afraid I cannot give you much help. We bought it, years ago in Europe, . . ." **Co** is 149 lines shorter than **Gh** and **Ot**. Twenty-two of these are missing from the start of the poem, where **Co** begins at l. 23. My guess is that originally the poem began on the verso of another text; and when the bookseller broke up the longer codex, he kept the earlier text complete thus shortening the poem. That decision may explain why the first gathering is seven folios, where eight would be expected after two larger sheets were folded to quarto size. The additional 117 missing lines (839-955) suggest that two leaves were cut from the MS at l. 839, for the second gathering has six leaves where eight would be expected. The change of speaker at l. 933 might account for the additional three missing lines.

**Me** Melk, Benediktinerstiftsbibliothek, MS 800 (olim 863) item 21, ff. 53r-63r, incipit: Claustralis vite quondam sanctissimus ordo. Paper, apparently good condition (seen online in a clearly reproduced copy), ff. 55r-63r, 205-215 x 145 mm, writing area 166 x 109 mm, 40 lines to the page, watermarks not visible in online reproduction, no catchwords, indeterminable collation, dated 1470 on f. 63r in the hand of the scribe who wrote the text, title in upper margin f. 55r: 'Dialogus persecutoris et zelatoris et vocatur flaccus poeta et est metricus.' The codex consists of theological and historical texts from the fifteenth century. See Christine Glaßner, *Katalog der deutschen Handschriften des 15. und 16. Jahrhunderts des Benediktinerstiftes Melk,* Katalog- und Registerband, Österreichische Akademie der Wissenschaften, phil.- hist. Klasse; Denkschriften 492 = Veröffentlichungen zum Schrift- und Buchwesen des Mittelalters III, 3 (Vienna, 2016), pp. 355-64. The scribe has either wilfully or carelessly omitted at sporadic intervals 915 lines apparently at random from a 1412 line poem, leaving a truncated version of 697 lines. He pays little or no attention either to the sense or to the metric requirements, causing both Hans Walther[23] and the **Gr** scribe a good deal of anguish. The hand is part book-, part cursive-hand, a German bastarda, and often careless. Single-compartment a; l, b, d, ascenders not usually looped; c and e often indistinguishable; m, n, u, usually distinguishable; both straight and round s, straight s descending below the baseline; r usually two-stroke, often confused with c and e; the shaft of t usually projecting above the headstroke; i occasionally dotted; g single-lobe and open lower bow; the limb of h descending below the baseline and curving slightly left. Often the readings in **Me** agree with those of **Co** against **Gh**, and I have adopted some of them, noted in the Textual Notes.

**Gr** Graz, Universitätsbibliothek, Graz, MS 1359, ff. 1r-8r (ll. 1-46, 589-1114) and 36r-40r, (ll. 95-504), paper, 200 x 150 mm, 16<sup>th</sup> century, catalogued in Anton Kern and Maria Mairold, *Die Handschriften der Universitätsbibliothek Graz*, vol. I (Leipzig, 1942; MSS 1-712), vol. II (Vienna, 1956; MSS 713-2066), vol. III (Vienna, 1967). Searchable catalogue at sosa2.uni-graz.at/sosa/katalog/index.php (accessed 6/3/21). Title on f. 2r: 'Dialogus duorum religiosorum alterius probantis et laudantis, alterius vero criminantis et reprantis iugum sancte religionis suave'. The brief codex has the following note on f. 1r: Rhythmi uarii a F Adamo Patzio Carthusiano priore Gemnicensi (= Gaming) collecti and contains the following poems: *Dialogus duorum religiosorum* (= LDM) ff. 1r-8r and 36r-40r; *Disceptatio vitae cum morte* ff. 9r-10r; *De fallaciis mulierum* ff. 10r-11r; *Carmina varia* ff. 11v-12v; *De contemptu mundi* of Bernard of Morval,[24] ff. 12v-33r; *De morte carmen horrendum* ff. 33r-34r; ff.

---

[23] Hans Walther, cited in note 5, pp. 167-8, notes the missing lines and mismetering and proposes that it might be a draft. He also counts 631 lines, where I have calculated 697 lines.

[24] The text is of all three books but lines are omitted, rearranged, and the three books are not separated from one another. The MS was not included in H.C. Hoskier's edition, *De contemptu mundi ... by Bernard of Morval* (London, 1929).

34v-35v blank. The text is a copy of **Me** with all its omissions, metrical errors and some additional ones unique to **Gr**; some classical orthography restored. Not used in this edition for it is not an independent witness to the text. The scribe is well aware of its shortcomings, for he comments on f. 8r: Inventio huius dialogi est valde bona, sed sensus plerisque in locis obscurus, constructio versuum et syllabarum quantitas contra regulas prosodie frequens. Num utrum aucthoris visio vel transcribentium negligentia contigerit, ignoro. Patet aucthorem eius fuisse virum doctum, et in rebus monasticis apprime versatum. Si quis dialogum totum corrigeret et elucidaret, haud ingratam religiosis zelatoribus rem fecisset.

About one hundred years lie between **Gh**, **Ot** and the manuscripts from the Upper Rhine area. Although all the manuscripts attest to the same poem, the small differences between the Flemish version and the Upper Rhine version suggest that the German/Austrian scribes tried to adjust the poem to suit local circumstances. The principal changes lie at lines 1147 and 1295-96. At 1147 the poet quotes a libellus addressed to Abbati Vacaranensi. There are two places with a name that could produce such an adjective, Vacaria/Vaccaria, a village called Vacquérie-le-Boucq in the arrondissement of Arras, Département Pas-de-Calais, and Vacaria/Vacheriae/Vacqueriae, a village called Vacquerières in the arrondissement of Alès, Département Gard, near Nîmes.[25] Neither of these villages, however, seems to satisfy the requirements for a monastery in the Middle Ages, for both are very small today (population respectively ca. 80 and ca. 300) and apparently have no ruins that might indicate the former presence of a monastery. But Vacquérie-le-Boucq at least agrees with both the catalogue conjecture and the hands, that the origin of the manuscript and perhaps of the poem lies somewhere on the border of northern

---

[25] Helmut Plechl and Sophie-Charlotte Plechl, *Orbis latinus: Lexikon lateinischer geographischer Namen des Mittelalters und der Neuzeit*, 3 vols. (Braunschweig, 1972-), s.v. Vacaria.

France and southern Belgium. The **Co** and **Me** scribes, however, either couldn't read their copy text or preferred to blur the origins of the poem, perhaps in order to make it fit with events closer to home. The **Me** scribe comes closest with vacaremensi, which would almost lead to Vacquérie-le-Boucq, but the **Co** scribe writes two words, uacare mensas, which might at a pinch mean 'may your table be empty.'

The changes at lines 1295-96 are more telling. **Gh** and **Ot** at that point read: 'maximus ille Iohannes/Gagetanus,' which in the context can only mean Pope Gelasius II (1118-19), Giovanni Caetani/Gaetani. Giovanni Gaetani was a member of the distinguished Italian family, the Gaetani/Caetani, which produced two popes: Gelasius II and Bonifatius VIII (1294-1303). The **Me** scribe omits lines 1285-1309, but the **Co** scribe substitutes 'uirorum' for 'Iohannes,' which opens the possibility that the line may refer to Pope Boniface, Dante's nemesis. All of which might be just mildly interesting except for a note in Stuttgart, ehemalige Hofbibliothek, MS XIV 20.1, f. 272vb, where we find the following:

> ... dar zü hat herzog Stephan ablas aller sunden gewunnen von dem vergangen pabst bonifatio auch alle octaw die in dem ganzen iar sind ...

The Stuttgart manuscript[26] deals chiefly with a life of St Michael and a life of Charlemagne, but on f. 267r ff there is a brief account of an imperial family: 'Von kaiser Cůnrat und gräf Leupolds sun Hainrichen. Da man zalt von Cristo geburt tausent und funfzehn iar czu den zayten reichsnet kaiser Chunrad.' Unfortunately the account does not go on to connect Herzog Stephan with the imperial family, but the rank of Herzog suggests that we are dealing with somebody of some account. Is it too far-fetched to suppose that the Upper Rhine Persecutor may have had connections of one sort or another with the family of Herzog Stephan? And clearly Boniface VIII is connected in some way, perhaps enough to make plausible the Persecutor's claim

---

[26] Described in *Die Handschriften der Württembergischen Landesbibliothek Stuttgart*, zweite Reihe, vierter Band (Wiesbaden, 1999), pp. 111-12.

Introduction xxvii

that the Pope just might come to his aid as he had done earlier. All that is speculation, for the evidence does not take us any further.

## THE ARTISTRY OF THE POEM

In addition to his skill with metric verse, our poet is also a gifted narrator, shaping his material artfully to give maximum effect to the order of events. First I think we must give him credit for creating—or perhaps reflecting—two distinct characters and for the psychological insight he brings to his task. Among her conclusions Cardelle de Hartmann[27] notes that the participants in dialogue texts exist only to exemplify the ideas or positions for which they stand. But our two monks differ from the norm in that each is a character, a personality in his own right. The Persecutor reminds me of a former colleague who was often involved in minor automobile accidents but was never at fault. So too the Persecutor inconveniently witnesses an abbot's arbitrary exercise of authority or is framed for theft by fellow monks, but defends his innocence strongly with a tone that verges on anger. The Zelator on the other hand is both a sympathetic listener and at the same time a calm but obstinate defender of the opposition. He finds excuses for bad behaviour, such as excusing, on the grounds of the irascibility of old age, the monk who threatened the Persecutor when he was ill (341-54). His admirable metaphor of builders rough-hewing their raw material into a building comes as a defence of an abbot who sent one monk into undeserved exile and drove a guest to suicide (614-722). Indeed, there are times when he seems to make the Persecutor feel he is batting a ball into a cushion. But there can be no doubt that the two debaters are distinct, even memorable, characters.

The angry and frustrated Persecutor begins his litany of complaint with strings of generalities and metaphors: monasteries are filled with fraud, deceit, malice, treachery of all sorts. He presents these complaints both with straightforward description and with figures of

---

[27] p. 263: ... die Personen sind nur dazu da, Inhalte zu vermitteln oder eine Diskussionsmethode exemplarisch vorzuführen.

speech, like a contrast of today's monastic life with the lives of the desert fathers (31-50) or four types of hypocrisy illustrated with invented characters (289-308) or envy described as a serpent divided in three parts (415-22).

The Zelator meets all these complaints calmly, almost placidly—as if the Persecutor were just running through a set text that he had heard before. His responses often reflect the complaints: for example the distinction between fraud and hypocrisy (375-84) or the serpent divided in three parts (497-502). For the most part, however, he poses biblical instances where one or another figure, mostly from the Old Testament, handled a similar situation differently. And the character that emerges is that of a calm, thoughtful and caring person, one sympathetic to the Persecutor though a bit too ready to pardon the abuse of authority. He is admirably equipped to counter the Persecutor's outraged conclusions with wise saws and witty instances. In fact more than once the Persecutor accuses him of being willing to find excuses for all sorts of misbehaviour (71-2, 157-8, 259-266, 403-8).

But finally the Zelator's patience wears thin, and he demands instances rather than generalities and rhetoric (589-94), and the Persecutor responds that he can tell of three abbots under whose guidance he developed all his resentment. These instances begin at line 599 and continue through the rest of the poem, with the first objectionable abbot described by quoting his treatment of one of the brothers whom he disliked (615-58) and the brother's subsequent suffering in exile (677-90). He goes on to describe the treatment of a guest to the monastery whom the abbot drives to a watery grave (693-722) and the abbot's punishment of the Persecutor for, apparently, appealing the abbot's behaviour to Rome (727-52). We never do find out the result of that episode, for the Zelator intervenes to express sympathy but also to exonerate the abbot. Here he elaborates an image of raw materials converted into finished products by potters, tilers, masons, and carpenters. We are the raw materials and our superiors those who coerce us into shape, sometimes with rough methods (771-804). I have never come across a similar set of images in medieval literature, and they are most effective.

## Introduction

The second vicious abbot was one who believed two of the brothers rather than the Persecutor, who accuses the brothers of having stolen a clasp to the abbot's cloak, the cloak itself, and the rain cape of one of the women who were cleaning and polishing the clasp. The women took the blame and sought some means of borrowing reparation from a usurer, but the brothers fixed the blame on the Persecutor (861-84). And of course the abbot believed the brothers, denying the need for evidence, and accused the Persecutor not only of theft but also of having fondled the women (885-99). No trial except the judgement of the mob is described, but the Persecutor anticipates exile.

The Zelator becomes increasingly sympathetic, even going so far as to criticise the abbot and asking the Persecutor how it all began, what was the root of all these troubles. And here the poet manages to do two things at once: he writes a flashback to illustrate how it all did begin and at the same time introduces the third evil abbot. This account opens with the story of Symon, a brother who turns out to be a thief and manages to ferret away a good bit of the treasure he collected, ostensibly to build a new foundation (1003-76). The Zelator at that point is all sympathetic ear and counters with a tale of an avaricious monk from his own monastery (1093-1128), ostensibly to suggest that Symon's evil may have stuck here and there to the Persecutor when he returned to his own monastery. But the Persecutor tells once again of how he was framed, this time by Symon (1147-1208), and once again the abbot believes the accusations without proof (1209-46). But first it is dinner time, and the abbot must eat. As luck would have it, he chokes on his dinner and dies well before he can administer any punishment (1251-64), and at that point a messenger arrives to say that Symon has been captured and he (the messenger) has come in search of the treasure Symon still presumes is his (1266-90). The figure of speech here (1267-8): Pontificem narrat Laphitarum cede peremptum/Symona captiuum carceribusque datum. (He reports that the bishop had been killed in the slaughter of the Lapiths and that Symon had been captured and jailed.) This turns out to be untrue, for actually Symon has sent his servant to reclaim all he has stolen. Somehow the reference to the Lapiths negates the capture and jailing of Symon, though I do not see how. But despite the Persecutor's feeling exonerated and ready for a tourist's visit to Rome, we are not told how Symon's loot eventually finds its way back, either to Symon himself or to the monastery where it belongs.

We are not told because the focus remains on the Persecutor, who at this point chronologically is back near the start of the poem, having decided to leave the cloister. But the impetus of the imagery is forward, to see the Persecutor reformed and ready to return to his monastery. In the final few lines he sums up the moral he has learned: that life will 'ram her fish and chips down your gullet until you . . . like it'[28] and it doesn't much matter who does the ramming, Decius or Datianus, Pilate or Nero, or a series of inept abbots, for he is now no longer the rebel Cain but rather the favoured Abel.

So in some 1400 lines the poet has presented us with two distinct characters, a convincing discussion, a satisfactory conclusion. It is not a typical debate poem, despite Walther's having included it in his study of debate poems,[29] rather I would call it a Dialogue poem of consolation, two monks discussing a problem and reaching a moment of healing. Perhaps it would not be too great an exaggeration to call it the first instance of the talking cure.

## INFLUENCES

The poet's ability to handle elegiac distichs indicates some exposure to classical Roman poets, especially Ovid's *Ex ponto* and *Tristia*. Despite the name Flaccus assigned to him in **Me**, I can find only a single line quoted from Horace, l. 945, a line quotable enough that he might have found it in a school text or a florilegium. He seems also to reflect a good bit of the *Aeneid*, especially book 6. The extremes suffered by the Persecutor make references to cold and uncomfortable places understandable and thus the exile in Ovid's poems wholly appropriate. He is also inventive when it comes to quoting the despicable abbots,

---

[28] Samuel Beckett, *Watt* (N.Y., 1959), p. 44.
[29] Hans Walther, as cited in note 5.

for some of their speeches are highly rhetorical, even opaque (617-58, 739-52), and I give him full credit for the extended metaphor of artisans shaping their raw material into finished products. Superb work? Probably not. Competent and imaginative? Definitely.

But conscience also requires me to note that not all apparent references to classical poems are dependable evidence that the poet has actually read the classical poem. He may well have come across quotations in a collection somewhere. But for what it may be worth, this is a tally of the references I have noted in the Explanatory Notes:

| | | |
|---|---|---|
| Ovid, | *Metamorphoses* | 6 |
| | *Tristia* | 6 |
| | *Ex ponto* | 3 |
| | *Ars amatoria* | 3 |
| | *Remedia amoris* | 2 |
| | *Fasti* | 1 |
| Vergil, | *Aeneid* | 8 |
| | *Eclogues* | 1 |
| Juvenal | | 4 |
| Statius, | *Thebaid* | 1 |
| | *Achilleid* | 1 |
| Horace | | 2 |

But as might be expected of a medieval Christian poet, biblical references abound, the Old Testament scoring some 52 citations to the New Testament's 34. I suspect that this preference reflects the poet's recognition of a good narrative more than his religious convictions.

Other references identified in the Explanatory Notes are not meant to imply the range of the poet's reading. Rather they indicate a possible source of information that might well have circulated in other texts available to him. In all he seems to have been a well-trained and competent poet with a relatively modest frame of reference. And he has produced the sort of poem such a poet might produce: interesting, entertaining, enlightening—but certainly no masterpiece.

## MONASTIC LIFE

There are fewer accounts of monastic life during the Middle Ages than one would expect, given the constant presence of the church and its institutions in daily life. Peter Abelard's focus in the *Historia calamitatum* is Peter Abelard, and monastic existence figures only to the extent that it impinges on his own life. He tells in some detail of the irritation he caused among the monks of St Denis after his work on the Trinity had been condemned at the Council of Soissons, and he complains vigorously of the behaviour of the monks at St Gildas de Rhuys in Brittany, who he claims were 'far more savage and worse than Saracens'.[30] But in both cases Abelard's attention is not on the conditions of monastic life in which he finds himself but rather on the torment and injustice he had to suffer.

Eadmer presents Anselm not as a dynamic leader of a group of monks, though reading between the lines suggests that he probably was, but rather as one who modelled himself as closely as possible on Christian charity and taught gently, persuasively, and with patience. His advice seems always generated by a charitable disposition towards his fellow monks, but we are left to infer how the day-to-day running of the monastery was accomplished under his direction.[31] The early twelfth-century abbot Guibert de Nogent, on the other hand, presents himself as a naive and superstitious man, one upon whom the devil was constantly intruding, and who usually thought of himself and his situation before any other consideration. He accused Jews and Muslims of unspeakable practices and was quick to blame on jealousy the dislike he felt coming from his fellow monks. Moreover, he says little about his abbacy at Nogent, a few miles west of Laon, and seems to have left his monastery largely to run itself.[32]

---

[30] J.T. Muckle, *The Story of Abelard's Adversities* (Toronto, 1954), p. 57.
[31] Eadmer, cited in note 12 above.
[32] John F. Benton, ed., *Self and Society in Medieval France: The Memoires of Abbot Guibert of Nogent* (1970; reprint Toronto, 1984). The whole memoire is a fascinating insight into one twelfth-century monk's personality, but he says little about the practical matters of running a monastery.

It is probably not surprising to discover from *Liber de duobus monachis* that conditions in a monastery look different to those in the midst of the scrum than they do to the abbots to whose attention the problems are brought. They are very like those in any "total institution"[33], where a group of people lead a life cut off from the wider society in an enclosed and formally administered life, where one's companions are unchanging from week to week and small annoyances can fester into serious sores. The smaller controlling group and the larger controlled group usually see one another in narrow and hostile stereotypes, and the larger controlled group often suffers from a sense of injustice, bitterness and alienation. The urge to vengeance must be, as *Liber de duobus monachis* attests, powerful.

## THE TEXT OF THE EDITION

**Gh** is the base manuscript for this edition. Since **Gh** and **Ot** are the only complete manuscripts of the poem, I have usually followed their readings. **Co** and **Mc**, however, from time to time offer readings that seemed to me to clarify an ambiguity or correct a grammatical error, and I have not hesitated to adopt readings from those manuscripts where appropriate. Where the Flemish and the Upper Rhine versions differ markedly, I have printed lines from both, for it seemed to me that the **Gh** and **Ot** scribes were more circumspect in their descriptions of excremental imagery, **Co** and **Me** more direct. Editorial additions are enclosed in pointed brackets, < >, and editorial deletions are enclosed in square brackets, [ ]. Punctuation, an editorial addition, has been kept to a minimum. Om signifies 'omit(s)'.

---

[33] The expression is taken from Erving Goffman, *Asylums: Essays on the Social Situation of Mental Patients and Other Inmates* (London, 1987; originally published 1961). See also Michel Foucault, *Surveillir et punir* (Paris, 1975; 2nd ed. 1993).

# THE BOOK OF THE TWO MONKS
## *OR*
## A DIALOGUE OF A CRITIC (THE PERSECUTOR) AND A DEFENDER OF RELIGIOUS LIFE (THE ZELATOR) AND THE POET IS CALLED *FLACCUS* AND THE POEM IS METRICAL


## LIBER DE DUOBUS MONACHIS
## &lt;VEL&gt;
## DIALOGUS PERSECUTORIS ET ZELATORIS RELIGIOSORUM ET VOCATUR FLACCUS POETA ET EST METRICUS

---

Title: The title is taken partly from **Gh**, f. 155r, partly from **Me**, f. 55r, the latter giving the names of the two monks conversing, Persecutor and Zelator. The name Flaccus for the poet is odd. There were three Roman poets called Flaccus, Quintus Horatius Flaccus (Horace, 65 BCE-8 BCE), Aulis Persius Flaccus (Persius, 34-62 CE), both satirists, and Gaius Valerius Flaccus (45-90 CE), whose *Argonautica* was lost until 1411 and is thus an unlikely model for a fourteenth century poet. At l. 945 Q. Horatius Flaccus is quoted (*Epistles* 1, 11, 27), and there are occasional other fragments noted here in the Explanatory Notes. Perhaps the poet's name or nickname really was Flaccus.

---

Title: **Gh**: title in lower margin, f. 155r, Incipit liber de duobus monachis, second hand (**Gh2**) as are almost all marginal comments. **Ot** untitled. **Co**: untitled. **Me**: title top of leaf, f. 55r: Dialogus persecutoris et zelatoris religiosorum et uocatur Flaccus poeta et est metricus. **Gr**: f. 2r, Dialogus duorum religiosorum alterius probantis et laudantis alterius vero criminantis et reprantis iugum sancte religionis suave.

Once upon a time the most holy order of monastic life had fostered two monks in religion. Right from his entry into monastic life, one of them would see a multiplicity of good things. But the other one, for whom no time was ever propitious, a man who, when they changed his monasteries, when he left various cloisters behind, saw with courage a multiplicity of public places. An unfortunate man, a pilgrim, constantly on the go, here holds forth and considers why he left the cloistered life. My writing speaks on his behalf. (10) It reports that a slender lad put aside the powerful weapons of Saul (nature herself teaches him this) lest he wish himself drawn under the yoke of someone else when he could be on his own—filled with pleasures and not yet burned by the fire of religious discipline. Yet he persuades himself to bear the monastic yoke, and that most spacious Bible arms him with its sacred text, with which at the same time he may argue his position.

Rather sharply then the two monks take their positions with arguments and do their utmost to carry off the prize of their dispute. I am the third participant, for I have been down the same road, (20) ploughed the same furrow, with the same fervour.

So I said: 'tell us, you two, the deep mysteries of the cloister, say what you want, and I will not allow you to hide anything. Believe whatever may be, I am your Homer and your Ovid and will sing your story widely. Nor will you, in my opinion, say anything unworthy of my song or that will not be pleasing in its sacred novelty. Meanwhile, the man for whom the monkish cell was more hateful than death now loosens his tongue, he

*Liber de duobus monachis*

Claustralis uite quondam sanctissimus ordo     f. 155r [olim 154r]
   Imbuerat monachos religione duos.
Unus ab introitu bona plurima uideret ipso.
   Alter, cui fuerat prospera nulla dies,
5  Qui, loca dum mutant dum claustri septa relinquunt
   Dissimiles, animo publica strata uidet
Multa, uir afflictus cursit peregrinus in orbe
   Disserit et quare claustra relinquat habet.
Prebet ei scriptura mea que fortia Saulis
10    Arma leuem puerum deposuisse refert
(Hoc et eum natura docet) ne sub iuga duci
   Se uelit alterius cum suus esse queat
Deliciis plenus nec religionis ab igne
   Vstus adhuc, suadet claustra iugumque pati,
15 Armat et hunc sacro latissima Biblia textu
   Defendat partem quo simul ipse suam.
Acrius ergo duo dum sic rationibus instant
   Et satagunt litis ferre trophea sue.
Tercius accedo nam calle ferebar eodem
20    Ruricolam simulans singula mente uera.
'Dicite claustrales secreto pectore,' dixi     f. 155v
   'Dicite quod uultis nec latuisse sinam.
Credite quidquid erit, ego uester Homerus ubique
   Uester et Ouidius, illud in orbe canam.
25 Nil, puto, dicetis quod non sit carmine dignum
   Vel quod non sancta sit nouitate placens.'
Interea tali linguam sermone resoluit

---

9–10 I Reg 24:9–19.

1–22 om] Co | 4–5] Me, a rubric inserted between lines 4 and 5 to summarise ll. 5–16, first word in red: Rubrica Nota quod illi duo simul conuersant ¶ temptatus autem dicit se velle deponere iugum sicut Dauid arma Saulis Alter uero suadet nullo modo Et dum simul contendent adest poeta qui dicta eorum metrice composuit vbi simul temptatus temptatus [sic] et quietus monachus disputant | 5–16 om] Me | 9 mea] uiam Ot | 17] om duo Me | 20 uera] noto Me, note Ot | 21–26] om Me | 23 incipit: Credite quicquid erit] Co | 24 orbe] ore Co

who in his own judgement suffered much unjustly, (30) as he first donned the potent insignia of the cloister.

**Persecutor:**
So what do you think of the monks and the novices of the cloister, those whom the final hour of this period brings forth? You don't imagine, do you, that they could be equal to the monks of yore whose names they read written in their cells? Do you suppose they are capable of reaching the sacred goals which such great men once reached? I certainly don't think so, but however much evening fades away from morning and day itself differs from night, by so much do they differ from those whom earlier ages (40) saw shining with holy signs.

The desert fathers endured many things: they existed in lonely places, they lived simple chaste lives, they scorned feasting and suffered very great hunger. To eat cooked food was to indulge in luxury. They spurned idleness; food which their own care-worn hands had not seasoned lacked flavour. They were wakeful in prayer, fervent in charity, admirable in their customs, serious in their religion. Nothing phony crept into them, but there was a heat of simplicity (50) as strong within as without. See if the monks these days, whose hearts are bitter beneath their goatskin clothing, resemble them.

Turning these things over in my heart, I said, 'Alas, how that excellent outward appearance has changed!' So what am I to do in the cloister? There is no perfection there nor any pious reflection of the holy fathers.

---

32 Ultima ... hora = Doomsday. The ultimate source is Apoc, but also cf. Bernard of Morval, *De contemptu mundi*, ed. H.C. Hoskier (London, 1929), l. 1. | 41–50 There are many accounts of the Desert Fathers, of which one of the most convenient remains Helen Waddell, *The Desert Fathers* (London: Constable, 1936; frequently reprinted).

---

29 inmerito] immeritis **Co** | 29–30] om **Me** | 31] The speaker is identified in **Co** only with ambiguous marginal abbreviations, e.g.: impg, ip, impi (Persecutor), la, ze, zel (Zelator), **Gh** prefers 'deprecator' for the critic, while **Me** uses 'Persecutor', which I

Cui sacra cella fuit morte perosa magis
Qui multa inmerito fuerat, se iudice, passus
30  Vt primum claustri fortia signa tulit.
**Persecutor:**
Quid tibi de monachis claustrique uidetur alumpnis,
  Ultima quos huius temporis hora parit?
Anne putas ualeant patres equare priores,
  In cellis quorum nomina scripta legunt?
35 Posse putasne sacras illas contingere metas
  Olim tam celebres quas posuere viri?
Non puto set quantum primo de mane recedit
  Vesper et a nocte discrepat ipsa dies,
Sic hij discordant ab eis quos secla priora
40  Viderunt signis irradiare sacris.
Multa tulere patres heremi: deserta colebant   f. 156r [olim 155r]
  Viuebant castis simplicibusque modis
Spreuerunt epulas, ieiunia summa ferebant.
  Sumere quid coctum luxuriasse fuit,
45 Otia pellebant, cibus ille sapore carebat
  Quem non condiuit fessa labore manus.
In precibus uigiles, in amore fuere calentes,
  Moribus insignes, religione graues.
Nil fictum subrepsit eis sed simplicitatis
50  Qui fuit exterius, hic color intus erat.
Aspice si tales monachi sint temporis huius
  Qui sub melotis fellea corda gerunt.
Hec in corde meo recolens, 'heu quomodo,' dixi,
  'Est immutatus optimus ille color.'
55 Ergo quid in claustro faciam? Perfectio nulla
  Est ibi sanctorum nec pia forma patrum.

---

have adopted | 32 huius] hus **Gh**; huius **Co, Me, Ot** | 34 cellis] celis **Co, Me, Ot**; legunt] leguntur **Me** | 35 illas contingere] illos **Gh, Ot**, attingere] **Ot** | 42 Viuebant] Viderunt **Me** | 44 Sumere] Summere **Me** | 46] om **Me** | 49 fictum] feclum **Gh**, fictum **Co, Me, Ot**, Nil] Nec **Me** | 50 color] calor **Co** | 53–54] om **Me** | 56 ubi] ibi **Co, Me, Ot**, Zelator] speaker unidentified **Gh, Ot**

**Zelator:**
O you who are precious to God, don't be pleased to retreat from the cloister and go backwards. I am running straight along the path I began—(60) it's shameful not to stick to the road you started on. We are running along the race-track: but only by finishing the race will each contestant rejoice to bring home his own prize. If a gladiator is fighting on the yellow sands of the arena and wielding his weapons against fierce beasts, let him fight and threaten with his drawn sword—if he doesn't win let him get no prize. Don't you recall how Lot's wife turned into a pillar of salt and what the stupid ploughman had when he looked behind him? Thus a dog returns to his puke and vomit, (70) and a sow wants to head back to her filthy pit.

**Persecutor:**
Why are you ready to hold me back with your words and harass me when I'm on my way? Me, I shall not stay in the cloister any longer. Fraud, guile, impiety, deception, pretence, envy, and whatever other monsters savage Megara produces—like hypocrisy, simony, pride, lust—these are the things that skulk there as in no other place. The contagions of these crimes rush past other places, but here they have a perpetual right to reside. I shall illustrate, taking instances from my own pain, (80) for everyone knows how to complain about his own problems first of all.

I was a youngster of promise, well suited to all sorts of virtue and to the ways of learning. I saw some monks, began to take notice of those I saw, and that pale crowd beguiled my sight. I approached closer, I

---

60 Cf. LSSM, p. 15, no. 185. | 61–62 Cf. I Cor 9:24. | 67–68 Gen 19:26 tells of Lot's wife turned into a pillar of salt, and Luc 9:62 quotes Jesus to the effect that a ploughman who gives up the plough is not fit for heaven. | 69–70 Prov 26:11 and II Petr 2:22. | 74 Megera. Cf. Vergil, *Aeneid*, 12, 846. Claudius, *De raptu Proserpinae*, 3, 387.

---

57] om **Me** | 58 Deo] Dei **Co**, rubric: ffrater zelans religionem sic respondit **Me** | 59

**Zelator:**
A claustro revocare pedem retroque reuerti
    Non tibi complaceat, vir preciose Deo.
Curro per inceptum directo tramite callem—
60    Est pudor inceptam deseruisse uiam.
Curritur in stadio: sed non nisi calle peracto
    Gaudebit brauium quisque referre suum.
Dimicet in flaua quamuis gladiator arena,
    Et cum dentata conferat arma fera,
65    Dimicet et stricto quantumlibet ense minetur—
    Ni tamen euincat premia nulla feret.
Num recolis salis effigiem Loth coniugis et quod
    Visus retrogrado stultus arator habet?
Sic canis ad vomitum fusasque reuertitur escas,
70    Sus ita pollutos uult repetisse lacus.

**Persecutor:**
Quid retinere paras uerbisque moraris euntem?
    Amplius in claustro non remorabor ego.
Fraus, dolus, impietas, simulacio, fictio, liuor,
    Et quidquid monstri torua Megera parit—
75    Scilicet ypocrisis, symonia, superbia, luxus—
    Hoc et non alio delituere loco.
Pretereunt alios scelerum contagia cursim,
    Hic sibi perpetue ius stationis habent.
Auguror a proprio sumens exempla dolore,
80    Quilibet in primis scit sua dampna queri.
Indolis egregie fueram puer, aptus ad omnes
    Virtutum species ingenijque uias.
Claustrales uidi, uisos attendere cepi.
    Decepit uisus pallida turba meos.

---

Curro] Cur **Co**, Curre **Ot** | 60 deseruisse] non tenuisse **Co, Me** | 62 brauium] quis brauium **Me** | 63 quamvis gladiator] quantumlibet actor **Co** | 63–66] om **Me** | 65 quantumlibet] quamvis satis **Gh**, quamvis **Ot** | 67 quod] quid **Me** | 68 retrogrado] retrogrados **Gh** | 70 repetisse] lacessis **Co** | 71 moraris] lacessis **Me** | 74 Megera] glossed furia **Ot** | 75–77] om **Me** | 77 scelerum] scelera **Co**

examined the depths of the life. I found there few men without some taint of sin. Bearded thieves, who have as many purses as their beards have whiskers, have become impious. Quarrelling stirs up the monks, anger provokes their superiors, (90) who, once offended, maintain a long-lasting split. Let's say that you have annoyed your abbot with some hand signal: the prior can't make peace between you. Or perhaps you've also offended a prior with some prank: the brothers can't reconcile you to him. Once you start being guilty and have fallen into error, you will never be able to get back up again—believe me. An angel with orders of anger against the people can be deflected with a sacrifice of good frankincense. If you have sinned in some way and are praying for forgiveness, (100) no sacrificial victim will purge your guilt. This impiety and most heinous error, alas, is now an inveterate plague in my cloister.

What then are the humble younger monks to do, among whom few bonds of peace remain? I have seen monks fighting furiously through their cloisters with their hair all dishevelled—and visible traces of blood remained on them. But The Book rather than a sword shed the blood. Some rushed for stones, others hoisted benches, (110) but the winner was the one who laid hands on The Book.

Prophetic scripture forbids such discord; it dismisses the people who want savage conflict. Abraham caused the wells of Gerara to flow with

---

108–10 It is difficult to see just how a book might serve as a weapon on a par with stones or benches/stools, but see Jay Diehl, "Origen's Story: Heresy, Book Production, and Monastic Reform at Saint-Laurent de Liège," *Speculum*, 95 (2020), 1051–86, esp. 1051–62 on the production of large codices, one of which might well have served as a weapon. | 113–14 Gen 21:30 and 13:8–11.

85  Amplius accessi, uiteque profunda probaui.
       Inueni paucos hic sine labe uiros.
    Fures barbati conuersi sacrilegi sunt,
       Qui tot habent loculos quot sua barba pilos.
    Lis stimulat monachos, exasperat ira patronos,
90     Quos semel offensos scismata longa tenent.
    Esto quod abbatem signo digitoue molestes:
       Hunc tibi non poterit conciliare prior.
    Offendas eciam quavis leuitate priorem:
       Fratres non poterunt te reparare sibi.
95  Cepisti semel esse reus lapsusque fuisti,
       Amodo non poteris surgere—crede michi.
    Thuris et incensi poterat libamine flecti
       Angelus in populum iussa furoris habens.
    Peccasti quocumque modo ueniamque precaris,
100    Purgabit culpam uictima nulla tuam.
    Hec est impietas multumque notabilis error,   f. 157v
       Pro pudor! in claustro pessima plaga meo.
    Quid facient igitur humiles monachique minores,
       Inter quos pacis federa pauca manent?
105 Vidi ego contorto monachos confligere pugno
       Et male distractas per sua claustra comas—
    Sanguinis hic eciam uestigia nota manebant,
       Set quem non mucro fuderat immo liber.
    Pars ad saxa ruit, pars altera scamna leuabat,
110    Cui liber euenit, promptior ille fuit.
    Tales conflictus prohibet scriptura propheta,
       Dissipat has gentes que fera bella uolunt.
    Liquit Abram puteos Gerare Loth federa liquit,

---

90 scismata] odia Co, Me | 91 signo digitoue] digito signoque Co | 91–94] om Me
93 quavis] quemvis Co | 96 crede] credi Me | 97–102] om Me | 99 quocumque]
quicumque Co | 102 pudor] dolor Co, pessima plaga meo] pestis adulta modo Co
103 facient] faciant Co, Me | 104 manent] marcent Me | 105 contorto] contortos
Me | 106–08] om Me | 110–12] om Me | 110 euenit] abuenit Ot, promptior]
sanctior Co

water and dissolved his bond with Lot, thus tolerating neither the power of the shepherds nor his own conflicts.

**Zelator:**
For various reasons conflicts befall even holy people. Bonds of lawful peace hold cloisters together. The peace of sinners does not exist there; it stands a good way off from holy houses and sacred monasteries. Didn't Abraham, the first father of our faith, (120) insult the kings in redeeming Lot? Right from the very beginning, not just from the creation of the earth, evil joined to good held no peace for anyone. You should know about angelic customs and learn about their battles: how the dragon fought with Michael.

And so there are those who disturb the devout silence of the monastery, who create schisms and want aggressive conflict. When the golden calf was presented to the people of the Lord, Moses seethed with fury and drove the guilty away. He said to his comrades, 'Go, strap on your swords, (130) smash a pathway of death through the people, let not friend spare friend nor acquaintance spare acquaintance, dedicate your hands against your own brothers.' Sometimes that's how the right correction punishes the guilty and how the anger of prelates strikes the wicked. And the dunces whose correction is severe cannot bear it with equanimity, so either they take up arms or in a malevolent rebellion they resist their superiors with quarrelling and anger and threats. What would Moses, the bold prelate, do to them then? (140) Would he abandon his own justice in such a way? I don't think so. Rather he would send his faithful friends into battle and he would enforce peace by means of a prison, a cudgel, a crucifixion.

---

119–20 Gen 14:13–16. | 121 For the distinction between the initium and the origo mundi, see Augustine, *De civitate dei*, 11: 9, ed. Emanvuel Hoffman, libri I-XIII, CCSL 40 (Prague, Leipzig, 1899), pp. 522–25; and PL 41: 323–25. | 124 Apoc 12:7–9. | 127–42 The legifer is Moses, the lawbringer; cf. Ex 20–23. Moses commands slaughter, Exod 32:27–28, as punishment for those who worshipped the golden calf.

---

117 peccatorum] precatorum Ot, est] om Ot | 117–20] om Me | 119 primeuus]

Nec vim pastorum nec sua bella ferens.
**Zelator:**
115 Casibus ex uarijs incumbunt prelia sanctis,
    Legitime pacis federa claustra tenent.
Pax peccatorum non est ibi, stat procul ista
    Edibus a sanctis cenobijsque sacris.
Nonne pater fidei nostre primeuus Abram
120     Regibus insultus Loth redimendo dedit?
Istud ab antiquo fuit hoc ab origine mundi,    f. 158r [olim 157r]
    Quod mala iuncta bonis non habuere fidem.
Celestes cognosce modos et prelia disce,
    Quomodo pugnauit cum Michaele draco.
125 Sunt ita qui turbant deuota silentia claustri,
    Scismata qui faciunt et fera bella uolunt.
In populum Domini uitulo prebente, furore[m]
    Legifer exarsit discutiendo reos.
'Ite,' ait ad socios, 'gladios accingite uestros,
130     Per medium populi rumpite mortis iter,
Non parcat notus noto nec amicus amico,
    Fratribus in proprijs sanctificate manus.'
Sic quandoque reos correctio digna flagellat
    Et prelatorum percutit ira malos.
135 Nec tamen id stulti quorum presumptio dura est
    Equanimi sensu sustinuisse queunt,
Vnde uel arma petunt uel seditione maligna
    Obstant prepositis lite, furore, minis.
Quid faciet Moyses prelatus strennuus istis?
140     Siccine iusticiam deseret ipse suam?
Non puto. Sed fidos in prelia mittet amicos    f. 158v
    Et faciet pacem carcere, fuste, cruce.

---

primarius **Co** | 121 ab antiquo fuit hoc] ab inicio fuit nec **Co**, hoc ab] ac **Me** | 122 non hubuere fidem] nil sibi pacis habent **Co**, **Me** | 123 Celestes] Angelicos **Co**, **Me** | 124 pugnauit] pungnat **Me** | 125 ita] ibi **Ot** | 126 et fera] non nisi **Co**, **Me** | 127 furore] furorem **Gh**, **Co**, **Ot** | 129–32] om **Me** | 133 correctio] presumptio **Gh** | 138 minas] nimis **Co**

Rarely it happens, however, that such a quarrel, aroused by stones, stools, The Book, may disturb chapter houses. But look at my face, take note of all my limbs, you will not find my head broken by a cudgel. I have not seen the brothers driven to fighting or to weapons: the cell is free for studies, the choir for praises. A turn around the cloister stops idle talk, monasteries get rid of sins, a (150) table bears food, a bed is for sleep. If you are peaceful and subject yourself to your superiors, your spotless reputation will erase your stain. Saul breathing threats of war and slaughter was rightly feared by the Lord's disciples. But when he learned to obey the teachings of the Thunderer, he stood out among the best of men.

**Persecutor:**
There is nothing so morally blemished that clever words will not polish it with the right efforts and skills. But for me neither the life nor the discipline of the cloister is suitable, (160) while that stink still lingers in my nostrils. There has always been only one proper order of life, capable of making all mortals righteous: namely, to scorn vice and love what is decent—nothing can be added to or subtracted from this. Nature provided this course from heaven for everyone. That law has a solidity from our Spiritual Father.

But now the world is full of monastic orders, and every land is held by hooded men: this fellow has a hermitage, that one a wooded retreat, another one lives in the country; (170) yet another one equips himself only for a noisy marketplace. A thousand different ways of life for men and a vast variety of vows, neither the words nor the deeds of one man please another. This character is brilliant, that fellow is worthless, the

---

153–54 Saul's many attempts to kill David and his many repentances are narrated in I Reg 19–24. | 160 Sap 2:2.

Fit tamen id raro quod lis capitalia turbet
    Talis quam stimulent saxa, scabella, liber.
145 Cerne meos uultus et singula membra notato,
    Inuenies fractum non michi fuste caput.
Non uidi fratres uel bella uel arma mouentes:
    Cella uacat studijs, laudibus ipse chorus,
Ambitus ora ligat, culpas capitolia purgant,
150     Mensa cibos librat, sompnia lectus habet.
Si sis pacificus tibi prelatisque subactus,
    Delebit maculam candida fama tuam.
Saulus adhuc spirans belli cedisque minarum
    Discipulis Domini iure timendus erat.
155 Ast ubi preceptis didicit parere Thonantis,
    Inter precipuos constitit ille viros.

**Persecutor:**
Est adeo deforme nichil quod callida uerba
    Non liment studijs ingenijsque bonis.
At michi claustralis nec uita nec ordo placebit,
160     Dum superest flatus naribus iste meis.
Vnus erat semper uite rectissimus ordo,    f. 159r [olim 158r]
    Cunctos mortales iustificare ualens:
Scilicet ut uicium spernatur, ametur honestum—
    Huic nichil apponi diminuique potest.
165 Omnibus e celo dedit hunc natura tenorem.
    A patre spirituum lex ea robur habet.
At nunc ordinibus est orbis plenus, et omnis
    Terra cucullatis est habita uiris:
Hic heremum tenet, ille nemus, rus incolit iste;
170     Non nisi clamoso se parat ille foro.
Mille uiris habitus et uoti discolor usus,

---

143 capitalia] capitolia Ot, turbet] stimulant Co | 143–44] om Me | 144 Talis quam] tales ergo Ot | 148 Cella vacat] cella vbi vacat Me | 151 subactus] subiectus Me | 154 iure] vir Me | 158 liment] leuiant Co, leniant Me | 161–66] om Me | 162 Cunctos mortales] Mortales cunctos Co | 168 cucullatis] cugullatis Me | 171 Mille viris] Est namque Me

third serves as a soldier, the fourth plays the prophet, another evaluates the food, while yet another judges just the vegetables.

Yet among these there are some for whom I have yet to see a suitable name—companions of fortune, people given to following secular courts. This lot softens the sharp bits while that one smooths the hard bits, gathering as much as possible to their clever trickery. Another man is always into trickery with some prince or other, (180) mixed in with the empurpled and the scarletted, he prays and orates like another Cicero; the whole ducal court hangs on his advice, and without it the king deals with neither great affairs nor even small ones, he doesn't establish peace nor does he wage wars.

Everything is done by monks with shaven heads, no court is without its clerics and its jesters. Often indignation distorted my face when I saw monks following blood-stained courts. 'Ach,' I said, 'what's going to happen? If monks follow the courts, (190) who will want to enter the cloister of Christ then? This is nothing other than promoting wars, spilling blood, burning houses in a flaming oven. Here a cow gets slaughtered, the one hope of a poor widow. Here a sheep that has just been snatched from the wolves has its throat slit. Don't touch such filth, stop it,' I said. 'Don't let this disgusting pillage stain consecrated men. Remember Tobias, see what he said, "If the animal has been stolen, I ask you to return it." Leave the secular courts far behind you, my brothers. Concentrate on the psalms. (200) Learn the blessed signs of a perfect man."

---

181 Tullius = Marcus Tullius Cicero (106 BCE – 43 BCE), the well-known Roman orator, statesman, and defender of the Republic. | 197–98 Tob 2:21.

---

172] om Me | 173 iste] ille **Co**, **Me** | 174 omne] omnem si **Me** | 175–78] om **Me** 177 Hoc . . . cautes] hos . . . cantos **Co** | 178 lucra sua] lucro suo **Gh**, **Ot**, **Co**. Second half line metrically deficient. | 179 hoc] hic **Co** | 182 curia tota] tota curia **Me** | 183 parua . . . tractat] et castra mouet nec prelia miscet **Co**, **Me** | 184 Nec . . . gerit] Filia non nubit nec sua sponsa parit **Co**, **Me** | 185 vertice] vertices **Me**, rasos]

Alterius nulli dicta uel acta placent.
Hic nitet, hic sordet, hic militat, iste prophetat,
   Judicat iste cibos, hic olus omne probat.
175 Sunt et in hijs nondum quibus apta uocabula uidi—
   Fortune socij, gens data castra sequi.
Hoc genus emollit cautes et saxa remulcet
   Colligit ingenio maxima lucr\<a\> su\<a\>
Semper in insidijs sedet hoc cum principe quovis,
180    Inter purpureos coccineosque viros,
Orat et eloquitur quasi Tullius alter; ab eius
   Consilio pendet curia tota ducum,
Hoc sine rex nec parua quidem nec grandia tractat,
   Nec pacem statuit nec sua bella gerit.
185 Omnia per monachos fiunt et vertice rasos,
   Fratribus et scurris curia nulla uacat.
Sepe michi toruum dedit indignacio uultum,
   Cum monachos uidi castra cruenta sequi.
'Ach, quid erit?' dixi, 'si fratres castra sequuntur
190    Quis modo pro Christo claustra subire uolet?
Non est hic aliud nisi bella mouere, cruorem
   Fundere, flammiuomo tecta cremare foco.
Hic bos mactatur, uidue spes pauperis vna.
   Vix erepta lupis hic iugulatur ouis.
195 Tangere pollutum nolite, recedite,' dixi.
   'Ne maculet sanctos sordida preda uiros.
Thobie memores estote, uidete quid inquit:
   "Si sit furtiuum reddite queso pecus."
Ite procul castris, fratres. Intendite psalmis.
200    Discite perfecti signa beata viri.'

---

rosas **Ot** | 186 Fratribus] Monachis **Me** | 187–88 Sepe michi . . . cruenta sequi] Quid fratres mei .nunc castra fouetis/Claustri deserti regula sicne iubet **Co** | 188 cruenta] uel arma **Co** | 189 Ach quid . . . sequuntur] Quid facitis fratres dixi num castra fouetis **Co** | 190 Quis . . . uolet] Claustraque deseritis regula sicne iubet **Co** | 191 om **Ot** | 194 Vix] Hic **Co** | 196 sanctos] uitam **Co**, uiros] sacram **Co** | 197 quid inquit] quod edum **Co** | 198 Si sit . . . pecus] Suspectum referat uxor amica monet **Co**

**Zelator:**
Death carries off the sick man for whom medicine has become poison, and the diseased eye clouds over in a bright light. In the same way there are those who never understand what is beautiful in holy orders, what is outstanding, or what is sacred in its seemliness. But they supply darkness to light, poisons for medicines, offer vice for virtues, filth for sweet spice. Since there are various sects throughout the world against which nobody either speaks or aggresses, why do you particularly dislike monks and those professing the cloister, (210) since they may number as many as the stars in the sky? Would you argue with a duke who drives off a rough enemy with six thousand troops? Doesn't the cloister seem to you God's outpost? Or Caesar's forces? And in the former one finds innumerable customs and ways of military service.

Who will Benedict's rule not save, as it drives out the stirrings of the flesh with thorns and briars? Try out what the Cistercians can do: you will be a travelling pilgrim—here there is much peace for you. Perhaps you want to defend the cross and the holy land with your sword, (220) then join the troops who bear the arms of the cross. Moreover, if you are weighed down with sloth, laziness, sorrow, the joyful white order will serve God. Perhaps the inappropriate cheering of the secular world assails you: you will find the Cistercian grove is a solitary hermitage. The order of Williamites is not frivolous: under their aegis are those who try everything and hang on to what is best. The holy order of Carmelites sails through the great sea and raises its spreading sails for heaven. And here are two brides, like two nourishing breasts: the Franciscans and (230) the

---

215–16 For an account of St Benedict in the briar patch, see Greg II, ii, pp. 78–79 (also in PL 66: 132.) | 215–30 In order: the Benedictines (215–16), the Cistercians (217–18), one of the orders of warrior monks like the Knights of St John of Jerusalem (219–20), perhaps the Premonstratensians or the Camaldolese Hermits of Mt Corona (221–22), the Carthusians (223–24), the Williamites (225–26), the Carmelites (227–28), the Franciscans (229), and the Dominicans (230).

---

202 aspectus] aspectum **Co, Me** | 205 lucem tenebras] tenebras lucem **Co, Me,**

**Zelator:**
Mors agit infirmum cui fit medicina uenenum,
    Lucis ad aspectus eger ocellus hebet.
Sunt ita qui nunquam sapiunt quid in ordine pulcrum,
    Quid sit conspicuum, quidue decore sacrum,
205 Sed ponunt lucem tenebras, medicamina uirus,
    Uirtutes vicium, cynnama munda fimum.
Cum sint diuerse mundi per climata secte,
    Contra quos nullus ora uel arma mouet,
Quid detestaris monachos et claustra professos,
210     Quod numero multi sint uelud astra poli?
Argueresne ducem qui cum sex milibus hostem
    Pelleret horrentem? Cesaris arma tibi
An non castra Dei tibi claustra uidentur? Et illic
    Mores innumeri milicieque modi.
215 Quem non saluabit Benedicti regula, carnis
    Expugnans stimulos uepribus atque rubis?
Conice quid possit Cystercius ordo: viator
    Aut peregrinus eris, hic tibi multa quies.
Ense crucem terramque sacram vis forte tueri,
220     Jungere milicie que crucis arma gerit.
Adde quod accidie segni merore graueris:
    Jocundus faciet candidus ordo Deo.
Forsitan impugnat te mundi plausus ineptus,
    Inuenies heremum Cartusiense nemus.
225 Wilelmitarum non est leuis ordo, sub isto
    Sunt qui cuncta probant et meliora tenent.
Montis Carmeli sacer ordo per hoc mare magnum
    Nauigat et celo stragula uela leuat.

---

uirus] morbum Co, Me, medicamina] medicina Ot | 206 cynnama] tymiamata Co, thimiama Me, munda] mundum Me | 207 mundi per] per mundi Co | 207–08 om Me | 208 nullus] nullius Gh | 210 Quod] Cum Me | 211–12] om Me | 212 horrentem] horrenti Co, Ot | 213 claustra uidentur] videntur claustra Me | 217–22] om Me | 218 tibi multa quies] tua rura metes Co | 219–20] appear after 223 Co 224 Cartusiensi] Cysterciense Co | 224–25] appear after 217 Co | 225–42] om Me

Dominicans have bowls of milk. They nourish your vision with examples and your understanding with words, nor do they cease to multiply new offspring.

You are a fine man and, dressed in a purple robe, you are resplendent: I on the other hand am freshly come to the arms of a sackcloth soldier. Would you do well to blame a physician with many pots of medicine who could perhaps help you when you are ill? Different diseases respond to different medicines, and one hand and one medicine box are not enough. Therefore, since the world is full of doctors and outside the cloister there is scarcely any well-qualified physician, who would forbid that one ask for or obtain some useful medicine out of all of them, one that each man approves for himself?

You also argue that the brothers frequent secular courts and stick to the advice of secular leaders everywhere. Believe me that in such matters this is not a mistake for those who are allowed to do it out of their own goodness. Furious kings, violent people, dukes would devour men alive and swallow the poor, (250) if the court were not supported by the brothers, by the gentle words and good advice of men. They defend the cause of the widow, they promote peace, they stand up for orphans, they inquire after the dying. Wasn't Herod said to have feared John and to have endured his good advice? And you, Elisha, Holy Father, who pleased the kings, through you the little field that had been taken from the Shunammite woman was returned to her. Moreover, no prey defiles that stomach which the splendid table of a clean heart nourishes.

---

**233** Ovid, *Ars amatoria* 2, 297, mentions an amictus Tyrius as a mark of distinction. **235–42** This is a general reference to medical doctors, but for a comprehensive history of medicine, see L.I. Conrad, Michael Neve, Vivian Nutton, Roy Porter, and Andrew Wear, *The Western Medical Tradition 800 BC to AD 1800* (Cambridge, 1995) and for the actual practice of medicine in the Middle Ages see Luke Demaitre, *Medieval Medicine: the Art of Healing from Head to Toe*, Praeger Series on the Middle Ages (Santa Barbara CA, Denver CO, and Oxford, 2013.) | **251–52** Cf. Ex 22:22, Deut 10:18, Ps 145:9, Ier 5:28, Iac 1:27. See also LSSM, p. 2, no. 35. | **253–54** Marc 6:20. | **255–56** IV Reg 8:1-6.

|     | Ecce duo sponse, uelud ubera plena: Minorum |
| --- | --- |
| 230 | Ordoque Maiorum pocula lactis habent. |

Exemplis oculos et uerbis pectora pascunt,
   Nec cessant fetus multiplicare nouos.
Comptus es et Tyrio fulges trabeatus amictu:
   Ad noua sacciferi militis arma veni.
235 An bene culpares medicum cum pixide multa
   Fortiter infirmo qui tibi ferret opem?
Dissimiles morbi medicamine dispare gaudent,
   Nec satis est vna pixis et vna manus.
Ergo cum medicis sit mundus plenus et extra
240 Claustrales uix sit phisicus arte potens,
Quis uetat e cunctisue postulet atque reportet ᶠ· ¹⁶¹ʳ [olim 160r]
   Utile pigmentum quod sibi quisque uidet?
Arguis hoc eciam quod fratres castra sequuntur
   Herent consilijs et quod ubique ducum.
245 Crede michi quod in hac re non erratur ab illis
   Permissum quibus est pro bonitate sua.
Sorberent homines uiuos inopesque uorarent
   Horrendi reges, gens uiolenta, duces.
Si non per fratres et uerba modesta uirorum
250 Consiliumque bonum curia fulta foret.
Defendunt causam uidue, pro pace locuntur,
   Stant pro pupillis, pro pereunte rogant.
An non Herodes fertur timuisse Iohannem
   Eius et hortatus sustinuisse bonos?
255 Redditur ablatus per te Sunamitis agellus,
   Helysee, placens regibus, Alme Pater.
Preterea ventrem non preda coinquinat illum
   Quem cordis mundi splendida mensa cibat.

---

234 sacciferi] facciferi **Gh** | 235 cum] de **Co, Ot** | 236 fortiter] fortis **Gh** | 238 vna pixis] vana **Co** | 240 uix] non **Co** | 241 cunctisue] quid nec **Co** | 245 erratur] eris **Me** | 247 uiuos inopesque uorarent] inopes viuosque vorantes **Co** | 248 uiolenta] uiolente **Co** | 252 pupillis] populus **Me** | 255–58] om **Me** | 257 preda] esca **Co**

**Persecutor:**
The blind man joyfully praise the meagre meal with his song (260), after the pepper and the whole hare came into his mouth. So, when everything is nicely done for you, you don't lament another person's tears or someone else's nasty fate. Everyone laments his own fate and is moved by his own sorrows and neglects everything else for expedience's sake. Even you, though I wish it were not so, when you are supervising each of your pupils, you are the one among them who is rightly feared. However, you may set up as an example for me Job, Noah, and Daniel—not even those three could keep me in the monastery. So you gain nothing by making excuses for the monks; on the contrary (270) you smear the vessel with pitch when the wave is about to recede. See how the fields are filled with much grain and see how many tiny atoms the orbit of the sun has—that is exactly the number of those in the monasteries who appear pious, sad hypocrites, pale mobs of the Styx. They are the pale faced creatures the angel points out in the Apocalypse, indicating each one in the shape of a horrible horse: 'I even saw,' he says, 'the fourth horse-face appear, whose rider was the image of death. All hell rushed behind him and followed after (280) and darkened the clear sky with black fire.' Who would not be deceived by such a pale ghost? When the crow pretends to be a swan and the wolf a sheep, when the thorn bush claims to be a lily and the reed a myrtle tree, when a gorse bush pretends to be spring roses—then we are all deceived; the ashes and sackcloth of hypocrisy and a celibate appearance carry little weight. This is the pollution that spoils the whole thing—a whited sepulchre on the outside, a stinking wasteland within. Alas! Hypocrisy, what disgust you have given me!

---

267 Ez 14:14. | 274 The river Styx in the underworld, mentioned among others by Vergil, *Georgics* 4, 480, *Aeneid* 6, 317-30. | 275–80 Apoc 6:7-8 | 282–84 Perhaps suggested by Vergil, *Eclogues* 8, 53-55. | 287 I Cor 5:6 and Gal 5:9. | 288 Cf. Matth 23:27.

---

263–66] om **Me** | 266 timendus] tenendus **Co** | 267 opponas] opponis **Co** | 269 nil . . . immo] non. . . ipse **Me** | 270–73] om **Me** | 270 Vnda . . . linis] Vda . . . ligas **Gh**, **Ot**, Vda vnda id est humida uel madida **Ot** (at foot of page) | 271 multa sint pleni gramina campi] densa stipetur arundine remis **Co** | 272 Quotque leues athomas orbita solis habet] Et quam multa celer saxa uoluta arax **Co** | 273 claustris] nobis **Co**

**Persecutor:**
Cecus ouans macram laudabat carmine mensam,
    Cui piper et totus uenit in ora lepus.
Sic tibi cum fuerint feliciter omnia gesta,    f. 161v
    Alterius lacrimas nec mala fata doles.
Que sua sunt querunt omnes propriaque mouentur
    Neglectis alijs utilitate rei.
Tu quoque, quod nollem, dum paruos quosque tueris,
    Unus ut ex illis rite timendus eris.
Attamen opponas michi Job, Noe, Danielem,
    Hi tres non poterunt me retinere loco.
Unde quod excusas monachos nil proficis, immo
    Vnda recessura cum pice uasa linis.
Aspice quam multo sint pleni gramine campi,
    Quotque leues athomas orbita solis habet—
Tot sunt in claustris speciem pietatis habentes,
    Ypocrite tristes, pallida turba Stigis.
Hi sunt pallenti quos signat in Apocalipsi
    Angelus, horribili quosque figurat equo:
'Vidi,' ait, 'et quartus facies exiuit equina,
    Ascensor cuius mortis ymago fuit.
Infernus post terga ruit retroque secutus,
    Fuscauit nigro sydera clara foco.'
Quem non decipiet fucati larua coloris?    f. 162r [olim 161r]
    Dum cignum coruus fingit, ouemque lupus,
Lilia dum rampnus simulat, myrtumque papirus,
    Mentitur vernas dum saliunca rosas,
Fallimur. Ypocritis cinis et sua barbara uestis
    Et celebs oculus non leue pondus habent.
Hoc est fermentum quod massam polluit omnem—
    Tumba foris lucens, tabe sed intus olens.
Proch dolor, ypocrite! michi tedia quanta dedistis!

---

275–80] om Me | 280 nigro] tetro Co | 281 fucati] fucata Me | 282 cignum coruus] coruum cingnus Co, Me | 283 myrtumque] uitemque Co | 283–86] om Me | 286 oculus] oculos Co | 288 tabe sed] tabeque Co

(290) But quickly to the point—that was your strong suit. You can divide this plague into four types, if you want to know how to avoid false brothers. The first kind wrinkles his brow and makes all sorts of fierce faces and gestures, a sad and down-turned mouth; puffed up in a hair shirt and sackcloth he wants to appear holy, but it is enough for him just to be a rough fellow among the unwashed. The second kind of wickedness differs from the first in that he is keen to please in behaviour; his face is cheerful, his words are witty, his (300) habits are modest, but he hides a huge heap of wickedness. The third type circulates and makes friends with everyone from whom he expects estates: some land in the country or some houses; to such people he may allow usury and stolen goods; justifying them he announces that they are equal to the saints. The fourth type of man looks for personal honours, and those he cannot have on his merits he tries to get by trickery. For this reason he flatters vice and entertains invidious whispers, and thus he fights for you, he approves of whatever you do. Woe is me! Wickedness! How I am oppressed by these men! (310) How much wickedness I have borne! And what great losses I have suffered!

Moreover, listen to my declaration in secret; don't let anyone else hear what things I complain about to you. Recently it happened that I was suffering from an acute illness, and I couldn't keep the food I had eaten on my stomach. This was the ailment that a physician calls vomiting—so those to whom the art of medicine is accessible have told me. I wasted away through loss of weight; pale death sat in my face; though sometimes my face turned red, then it turned as pale as boxwood. And since I languished for a long time and would have been of no use to my cloister,

---

317 Cf. Horace, *Carmina* I, 4, 13.

| | Sed breuis ad punctum gloria uestra fuit. |
|---|---|
| 290 | |
| | Quatuor in species potes hunc distinguere morbum |
| |     Fratribus a falsis posse cauere uolens: |
| | Prima supercilium corrugat et asperat omnes |
| |     Wltus et gestus tristis et ore grauis, |
| 295 | Cilicio saccoque tumens uult sancta uideri |
| |     Et satis est illi sordibus esse rudem. |
| | Altera nequitie species discordat ab ista |
| |     Quolibet in gestu posse placere studens; |
| | Est facies hilaris, sunt uerba faceta, modesti |
| 300 |     Mores, nequitie set latet alta strues. |
| | Tercia circumiens voto sibi federat omnes     f. 162v |
| |     A quibus expectat predia, rura, domos, |
| | Talibus usuras predamque licentiat, istos |
| |     Justficans sanctis predicat esse pares. |
| 305 | Quarta hominum species priuatos querit honores, |
| |     Quosque nequit meritis temptat habere dolis, |
| | Hinc uitium palpat, hinc blanda susurria tractat, |
| |     Hinc pro te pugnat, hinc tua facta probat. |
| | Ei michi, nequitias! Quot sum perpessus ab istis! |
| 310 |     Quot mala sustinui! Quantaque dampna tuli! |
| | Preterea, ausculta, mea clam tibi suscipe uerba, |
| |     Audiat hec nullus que tibi facta querar. |
| | Accidit hoc nuper quod acuta peste tenebar, |
| |     Nec poteram sumptos ore tenere cibos. |
| 315 | Ipse fuit morbus quem phisica dicit orexim— |
| |     Sic michi dixerunt ars quibus illa patet. |
| | Squalebam macie, mors pallida sedit in ore, |
| |     Et modo si qua rubet tunc gena buxus erat. |
| | Cunque diu languens claustro nichil utilis essem, |

---

291–94 Quotuor . . . grauis] Officia querit sed non vult talia sciri/Data recusat se miserum approbat ore/Mente tamen latet nam putat se optimum fore **Me** | 296–97] om **Me** | 297 nequitie] figmenti **Co** | 298 quolibet] quelibet **Gh** | 301 Tercia] Terras **Me** | 303 licenciat istos] vsuris istis **Me** | 304–06] om **Me** | 305 hominum] mali **Co** 308–12] om **Me** | 311 tibi] ti **Co** | 312 facta] fata **Gh** | 314–18] om **Me**

(320) everyone began to find me tiresome. The complaint went round that for all the small amount of medicine I had taken (less than two shillings worth in my opinion), the wretches charged me for meals and for a horrible attendant. They set before me something satirical they had conceived: a small fish might perhaps have fed me for two days, even though for them the big question concerned a turbot.

See how justly indignation about my illness provoked me! I don't know which Satan it was among them who said to me, 'Just lying there you are deceiving all of us. (330) You're healthy and bloated with honey, you're flowing with honeycomb. You are healthy and robust. This matter is going to go in another direction. There will have to be applause for a different game. By golly, if there were strength or sturdy power in my hands, I'd cure your illness with a cudgel, by golly. If I can't do it alone, the weapons of a judge will help me. A violent hand will put you outside the cloister.' I got away quickly, doing whatever it took. He led my whole convent with a threatening cudgel. And the man who did this was no cleric—on the contrary, (340) a bearded savage from the old days.

**Zelator:**
Just as playful games sometimes lack playfulness, so serious matters can often lack seriousness. Apart from everything else which I have examined as extreme examples, the anger of the bearded old man displeases me most. Come, tell me, what punishments did his abbot impose on him? Didn't he feed him on the bread of penance? He certainly deserved a punishment fitting the crime, but I'll bet your mercy forgave the old boy. Old men do many things that we don't usually punish: (350) a life made

---

325–26 The point of the comparison seems elusive. Perhaps an allusion to Juvenal, Satire 4, 37–154, on an enormous turbot presented to the Emperor Domitian.

322] om Me | 324 satiro] rustico Me | 324–25 between the lines Me adds] senem iratum barbatum impium malum | 326 et sibi de rumbo] etsi de rumba Co, Est sibi rumbo Me | 327–28] om Me | 328 Sathanas] Sathan Co | 329 dudum nos Gh, Ot

320  Ceperunt omnes tedia ferre mei.
         Murmur erat cunctis medice pro sumptibus artis
             Quos tamen ad solidos uix reor esse duos.
         Prandia taxabant miseri dirumque ministrum.
             Ex satiro genitum proposuere michi:
325      Paruula per biduum me fundula forte cibasset,
             Et sibi de rumbo questio grandis erat.
         Aspice quam iuste me commouet ira querele!
             Nescio quis Sathanas affuit inter eos
         Ille michi dixit, 'Discumbens decipis omnes.
330          Sanus es et fortis melle fauoque fluis.
         Grassus es et pinguis. Alijs res passibus ibit.
             Alterius ludi plausus habendus erit.
         Ercle! Uigor manibus vel si sunt robora pinguis,
             Curabo morbum fustibus, Ercle, tuum.
335      Si nequeo solus, me iudicis arma iuuabunt.
             Mittet pro foribus te uiolenta manus.'
         Protinus euasi cupiens quodcumque necesse est;
             Duxi\<t\> conuentum fuste minante meum.
         Qui tamen hoc fecit non clericus extitit, immo
340          Barbatus ueteres toruus adusque dies.
         **Zelator:**
         Vt ludi quandoque carent bonitate faceta,
             Seria nonnumquam sic grauitate carent.
         Dimissis alijs que singula dura probaui,
             Plus michi barbati displicet ira senis.
345      Dic, age, quas penas illi suus intulit abbas—
             An non angarie pane cibauit eum?
         Ille quidem penam meruit pro crimine dignam,
             Set tua subuenit gratia credo seni.

---

330] om Me; | 330–31] lines reversed in Gh | 331 grassus] grossus Co, Me | 333] om Me | 334 Ercle] ego Me | 335] om Me | 336 pro] pre Co, Me | 337 quodcumque necesse est] euadere minas Me | 338 duxi\<t\>] duxi Gh, Co, Me, Ot | 339–40] Om Me | 341 bonitate] leuitite Ot | 341–48] om Me | 345 age] ages Ot | 347 penam . . . dignam] dignam . . . penam Ot | 348 seni] sibi Co, tua] om Co

heavy with suffering grants mercy to the old. They often rave, and those whom they chase with a club today they want to embrace tomorrow with a hug of peace.

Oh what a joyful life I might have hoped to lead, if an old man had said such abusive things to me. Also even a young man might have said such abuse and threats to me; should my intent have been respected on that account?

Semey committed a shameful act scattering stones and dust in David's face; the king endured these curses and could then have sent doubled forces (360) to cut off the head of the mad dog. And the old man could have handed you, whom he mistrusted, over to all the others. Why on earth did you take his complaint so seriously? You ought to have hoped with all your heart to be raised to heaven, freely desiring to leave your earthly home. You have often heard of St Agatha, the martyr: she didn't use magic arts but only the word of God who transforms everything—she sought the help of a spiritual doctor.

Some medicine, powder mixed with pitch, does not agree with some men, (370) a leaf mixed with ashes, thyme mixed with senna. So let the ardour of the brothers please you for its generous intent, so go easy on the hard abuse of the old man. Words don't hurt much, unless perhaps a beating follows; a word is a trivial offense, bloodshed a much greater one.

---

349 Cf. Reg mon, cap. 37, "De senibus vel infantibus." | 350 Cf. Juvenal, Satire 2, 63: "Dat veniam corvis …" | 357–60 II Reg 16:5–14. | 365–68 For St Agatha see AASS Feb I, 662. | 370 Diasene, a compound medicine, is described in the *Antidotarium Nicolai* as valet … proprie multicis maniacis cardiacis: et tristibus … quod valet quartanaris et magis spleneticis. See Dietlinde Goltz, *Mittelalterliche Pharmazie und Medizin*, … *mit einem Nachdruck* [des *Antidotarium*] *des Druckfassung von 1471* (Stuttgart, 1976). The reproduction of the 1471 edition is unpaginated and unfoliated, but the compounds are listed in alphabetical order. Thymum = thyme is listed for its medicinal value in *Culpepper's Herbal* (reprint:

|       |                                                            |
|-------|------------------------------------------------------------|
|       | Multa senes faciunt que non punire solemus,                |
| 350   | Dat veniam senibus vita dolore grauis.                     |
|       | Delirare solent, et quos modo fuste sequuntur              |
|       | Pacis in amplexus mox repetisse uolunt.                    |
|       | O quam iocundam sperarem ducere uitam                      |
|       | Si michi dixisset talia probra senex.                      |
| 355   | Adde quod et iuuenis michi probra minasque dedisset,       |
|       | An fuit idcirco mens veneranda michi?                      |
|       | Probra dedit Semey, lapides cum puluere spargens           |
|       | In faciem Dauid; rex maledicta tulit,                      |
|       | Denique tunc poterat geminas misisse cohortes              |
| 360   | Et caput insani deposuisse canis.                          |
|       | Hoc et suspectum poterat te reddere cunctis.   f. 164r [olim 163r] |
|       | Quid tibi pro uita questio tanta fuit?                     |
|       | Debueras totis sursum sperasse medullis,                   |
|       | Sponte uolens luteam deseruisse domum.                     |
| 365   | Sepius audieras Agatha de martire sancta,                  |
|       | Que non peonijs artibus usa fuit                           |
|       | Sed solo sermone Dei, qui cuncta reformat—                 |
|       | Quesiuit medici spiritualis opem.                          |
|       | Displicuit medicina viris cum pixide puluis,               |
| 370   | Cum spodio folium, cum dyasene thymum.                     |
|       | Hinc fratrum zelus placeat pro sumptibus amplis,           |
|       | Hinc laxanda tibi sint probra dura senis.                  |
|       | Uerba nocent modicum, nisi uerbera forte sequuntur,        |
|       | Culpa leuis uerbum, maxima culpa cruor.                    |
| 375   | Fraudis et ypocrisis per te distinctio facta               |

---

Ware, Herts., 1985), p. 290, though it is not listed in *Ca. instans*. Spodium is listed in *Ca. instans*, f. 209v, where it is recommended for a nose bleed, a flux from dysentery, haemorrhoids and menstruation.

---

350] om **Me**, senibus] canis **Co** | 354–55] om **Me** | 355 proba minasque] uerba probrosa **Co** | 356 veneranda] uarianda **Gh** | 361–62] om **Me** | 363 sperasse] sperisse **Gh**, totus **Me** | 365–70] om **Me** | 366 que] quod **Co** | 372 sint] rogo **Co**, **Me**, om dura **Co**, **Me** | 374] om **Me**

In holy orders there is no distinction, like the one you have made, between fraud and hypocrisy, believe me. I know this great sin only from books, for every good order is free from that plague. I know what the letter says, but the interlinear gloss, (380) which tells us nothing, is fearful enough. So I fear for myself, lest while judging anyone badly, I shall be afflicted with the same malady.

Latins still don't know what hypocrisy was: it's a Greek word and a Greek nuisance. But there are among us those who work in poverty, who grow pale from a broken body, but who have a vigorous mind. Those who are always welcome and everywhere up to date are brought together with words and are suitable examples for our morals. Moreover, there are brothers here serving their cloisters (390) who are useful to themselves and a profit to others. I don't know anyone among them who seeks praise or honours for himself; he who lacks duties lacks grief. I don't think that anybody, if not compelled by his superior to do it, would apply himself to such duties voluntarily. I have often seen men with the keys and symbols of office prostrate themselves before the feet of magistrates; they wept copiously and asked to be let off, certain that the highest responsibility would incur the heaviest burden. Christ is a good example: raised to the high (400) summit of the kingdom, he rejected the sceptre and fled. Inspired by this example each cautious person will turn away himself, always seeking the lowest place.

**Persecutor:**
This is the most certain rule for those of us who are troubled: that we are both wretched jokes and objects of ridicule. Any mocker who turns

---

**399–400** Matth 4:8–11 and Luc 4:6–8.

In sancto non est ordine, crede michi.
Ex libris tantum uicium michi noscitur istud,
 Omnis ab hac purus est bonus ordo lue.
Litera quid dicat noui, sed glosa superstans,
380 Nullum notificans, est metuenda satis.
Unde michi timeo ne dum male iudico quemquam, <sup>f. 164v</sup>
 Ipsius morbi condicione premar.
Ypocrisis quid sit nondum nouere Latini,
 Est sermo Grecus, Grecaque pestis erit.
385 Sunt tamen in nobis qui paupertate laborant,
 Qui pallent fracto corpore, mente uigent.
Uerbis compositi sunt nobis moribus apti,
 Qui semper grati sunt et ubique noui.
Preterea fratres sunt hic sua claustra iuuantes
390 Qui sibi proficui sunt alijsque lucri.
Nescio quis laudes vel quis sibi querat honores;
 Qui caret officijs ille dolore caret.
Non puto quod quisquam sc talibus ingerat ultro
 Quem non prelatus cogit ad ista suus.
395 Sepe viros uidi cum clauibus atque sigillis
 Ante magistrorum procubuisse pedes,
Fundebant lacrimas, absolui seque petebant,
 Certi quod casum dant loca summa grauem.
Christus in exemplo est, qui raptus ad ardua regni
400 Culmina, deseruit sceptra deditque fugam.
Huius ad exemplum facti se quisque retorquet<sup>f. 165r [olum 164r]</sup>
 Prouidus, extremum semper amando locum.

**Persecutor:**
Hec est afflictis certissima regula nobis
 Simus ut et miseri ridiculumque ioci.

---

377 istud] illud Me | 378 Omnis . . . lue] Nec speciem nec habet regula nostra genus Co | 378–80] om Me | 380 notificans] mortificans Gh | 387] om Me | 395 viros] fratres Me | 396 magistrorum] prelatorum Me | 397 seque petebant] sponte nolebant Co, seque] sponte Me | 399 Christus . . . est] Exemplum in Christo Co, Me, potest . . . esse Ot | 401 facti] frater Me

something serious into a lighthearted joke deserves praise for his artistry. Even you should be considered not a monk but a comedian when you thus mitigate here a crime, there a sin. So you persevere with your art of jokery (410) and like a modern Amphion you would tame the very stones with your lyre. You don't do anything but spend your time in trivial studies, but no flattering flute is going to sing the cloister to me. What I have written I have written; I have seen no worse sorts than those in the cloisters and in holy orders.

Should I pass over in silence the plague of envy? There is no more malicious serpent lurking in the cloister. The dragon of envy, thrown down from high heaven, divides its being into three parts. Among laymen it forms the Haughty Head; (420) among secular clerics it perches in the Groin where it creates Lust, with which it drags down the stars. Among monks and those in holy orders it thrusts the Tail of Bitter Malice. Of heavenly origin envy is the old offspring of the gods—it wants to live only among the wealthy. Would you believe that the stuff that greedy envy refuses to seize is wholly vile, wholly feeble, wholly useless? The south wind blows its flames into the tall cedars as envy itroduces arms among illustrious men. You are a great man—and you could be greater or even the greatest, (430) but envy makes you small, smaller, smallest. Alas, this descent describes my fate, for my fate now grants me only a slow climb back up. I who entered the cloister a good man now leave it not such a good man. I have been sent forth a new bird in new feathers. Once a cedar, now I am just a useless bit of vine wood, cut down by a scythe and now given as fuel for the fire. Once praise made me taller than plane

---

410 Horace, *Carmina* 3, 11 sees Amphion moving stones with his song (canendo); *Epistulorum* 1, 18, 41–43, sees him building walls with his lyre; *Ars poetica* (*Epistulorum* 2, 3), 394–96 sees him building walls with the sound of his lyre and with proper prayers. See also Statius, *Thebeid* 1, 10. | 413 Ioan 19:22. | 426 liuor edax, Ovid, *Remedia amoris*, 389. | 435–39 The hierarchical order of trees is perhaps derived from Eccli 24:17–19.

---

405–06] om Me | 408 scelus] zelus Co | 409 Attamen] Attamen affif Me | 410 domes] trahas Co | 415 claustrum] claustro Co, Me | 417–33] om Me | 423 soboles

|405| Quilibet irrisor laudes hac arte meretur,
   Uertat ut in ludos seria queque leues.
Tu quoque non monachus sed eris derisor habendus,
   Dum sic attenuas hinc scelus inde nephas.
Attamen insistas quorumlibet arte iocorum,
|410|   Et nouus Amphyon pectine saxa domes.
Nil agis et studijs deducis tempora vanis,
   Nulla michi claustrum fistula blanda canet.
Quod scripsi, scripsi—peiores non ego uidi
   Quam sunt in claustris ordinibusque sacris.
|415| Inuidie taceam numquid contagia claustris
   Qua non liuidior anguis inesse solet?
Serpens inuidie celo proiectus ab alto
   In tria diuisit corporis esse sui.
In laycis fastum tanquam caput, inguina uentris
|420|   In clero posuit luxuriamque dedit,
Qua stellas traxit. Caudam liuoris amari     f. 165v
   Iniecit monachis ordinibusque sacris.
Celica stirps liuor soboles antiqua deorum—
   Non nisi cum diuis uult habitare viris.
|425| Uile uel infirmum credas uel inutile totum
   Quod dedignatur carpere liuor edax?
Eurus in erectas mittit sua flamina cedros,
   Et liuor claris ingerit arma uiris.
Magnus es et maior poteras uel maximus esse,
|430|   Hic facit ut paruus sis minimoque minor.
Pro dolor! Ista meis est apta gradatio fatis,
   Nam michi retrogrados dant modo fata gradus.
Qui bonus intraui iam non bonus exeo claustrum,
   Tales in plumas sic noua mutor auis.
|435| Olim cedrus eram, nunc uitis inutile lignum,
   Quod de falce cadens ignibus esca datur.

---

antiqua ] proles inuisa **Co** | 430 minimoque minor] minor et minimus **Co** | 432 Nam . . . modo] Non . . . michi **Co** | 434 Tales . . . auis] Talibus in plumis se mea mutat auis **Co, Me**, mutor] mittor **Gh** | 435 Me nunc] non **Me**

trees and cypresses—the fat olive tree yielded to my merits. Like a spring rose I was the picture of virtue, (440) and in my judgement I was worth more than any other. But now brought low, I am more wretched than anyone. When I try to get up, no one gives me a hand. Alas, in a celibate life there is no shoulder to cry on; there is no balm in Gilead for me. That no one has charged me with a crime—this alone assuages the wretchedness of an afflicted life. Perhaps some blemish of error sticks to me, for hardly a person is to be found who does not sin. A mistake can sometimes be helped with forgiveness, (450) but a crime will always find assistance tough. What more can envy add to my fate? Anyone on whom such things have once been piled—isn't he already buried? But I pity those whose names are still unblemished and who have seen a long period of service, those who now fall and abandon their habit and their monastery, as you see in my vow and resolution. Who would not ultimately pull back from the fire of envy? We are not bricks or ivory or salamanders. O with what speedy feet would this one and that one leap away, (460) even those I thought were the base and bones of the cloister.

The sharply-toothed animal that Daniel saw is said to have three rows of teeth in his huge mouth—he was a bear in appearance standing to the side, and they said to him, 'Arise, take action, arise you hungry creature! Now fill your mouth, fill it with blood, you infernal plague, devour an abundance of flesh!' Prelates and cruel masters are that beast, and like the bear they too have enormous arrogance. In their mouths there is a triple

---

444 Ier 8:22. | 448 Cf. LSSM, p. 37, no. 36; III Reg 8:46; Eccli 7:21. | 458 For salamanders and fire see Pliny, *De historia naturalia* 10, 188 (= LXXXVI). Ebanus = hebenus. | 461–66 Dan 7:5.

---

437–41] om Me | 440 dignus] pulcer Co | 441 modo . . . exto] nunc, esto Co | 443

Uincebam platanos, vincebam laude cypressos,
   Cedebat meritis pinguis oliua meis.
Ut rosa verna fui species virtutis, et omni
440    Plus alio quam, me iudice, dignus eram.
At modo depressus nulli miserabilis exto;   f. 166r [olim 165r]
   Surgere dum tempto, dat michi nemo manum.
Heu, consolator non est sub celibe cultu,
   Non est in Galaad ulla resina michi.
445 Hoc tamen afflicte solatur tedia uite,
   Quod de me crimen dicere nullus habet.
Forsitan erroris aliquis michi neuus inhesit,
   Nam qui non peccet uix reperitur homo.
Error habens ueniam poterit quandoque iuuari,
450    Crimen difficilem semper habebit opem.
Quid liuor fatis ualet amplius addere nostris?
   Quem semel exstruxit nonne sepultus erit?
Compatior tamen his quorum sunt nomina clara
   Et quos militie tempora longa uident,
455 Qui modo succumbunt habitumque locumque relinquunt,
   Cernis ut in uoto propositoque meo.
Quis non inuidie tandem resiliret ab igne?
   Non later aut hebenus uel salamandra sumus.
O quam precipiti pede transilit vnus et alter,
460    Quem claustri uectem rebar et esse basem.
Bestia quam uidit Daniel dentata fuisse   f. 166v
   Dicitur ordinibus ampla per ora tribus,
Ursus erat facie stans partibus e regione,
   Dicebantque sibi, 'Surge, age, surge uorax!
465 Nunc fauces diffunde tuas, satiare cruore,
   Carnibus innumeris uescere, dira fames.'
Bestia prelati sunt immitesque magistri,

---

cultu] uita Co, Me | 444–51] om Me | 444 Galaad ... michi] monachis prorsus habenda fides Ot | 451 fatis] fatus Co | 452 semel exstruxit] liuor extinxit Co, Me 453] om Me | 455 Qui] Et Co, En Me, Quo Ot | 456 Cernis] certus Gh | 457–58] om Me | 458 uel] aut Co | 461–66] om Me | 466 fames] lues Co

order: guile, violence, and envy—(470) with these teeth they gnaw and mangle their flock—the honest men with violence, the learned with guile, and the peaceful with envy, lest this one or that one gets too big for his breeches. Our abbots decree many laws well beyond the flapping sails of the Sarmatians. Let them make many laws—if by chance they feared they might be subject to them, then they wouldn't be quite so arbitrary.

They also recite obituaries of the brothers by name—those for whom an annual recitation formalises their leaving this life. For these dearly departed they read five thousand psalms (480) and twelve hundred Pater Nosters. Oh if I were pope or the greatest abbot of the fathers, I would offer such fat gravy just for the living! Naturally, I would wish that the names of all my brothers were recited right here, those whom the savage bears have chewed to bits, those who having been swallowed up by the envy of their superiors have now fled, lest they become food and drink for metaphorical wolves. To those afflicted I would offer tears, fasts, psalms, the singing of masses, incense, and prayers. This would then be a lament for the living (490) rather than for the dead, who have their place of rest. Finally grace only is owed to the dead; (470) something must always be done first for the living.

**Zelator:**
Anyone who denies all human life and customs will be brighter than the sun and whiter than snow; he will not be a resident of this polluted world but rather of the heavens or perhaps, Paradise, one of your citizens. A

---

473 Ovid refers to the Sarmatians often in both the *Ex Ponto* (e.g., 4, 10, 38;) and the *Tristia* (e.g., 2, 198; 3, 3, 6; 3, 10, 5; etc.) to mean the people living around the Black Sea (Mare Sarmaticum). By the time of Juvenal (*Satire* 2:1), late first/early second century CE, the phrase means something like the back of beyond, remote, cold, wild, etc.

Grande supercilium qui uelud ursus habent.
Ordo per ora triplix: astus, uiolentia, liuor,
470    Dentibus hijs frendent dilaniantque pecus—
Ui iustos, astu doctos, liuore serenos,
    Ne radiet titulis iste uel ille suis.
Ultra Saromatas longe sua carbasa flantes,
    Abbates nostri multa statuta parant.
475 Multa statuta parent, que, si fortasse timerent
    Esse tenenda sibi, non modo tanta forent.
Hic eciam recitant obitus et nomina fratrum,
    Dant uite excessus annua fata quibus.
Hijs pro defunctis psalmorum milia quinque
480    Atque 'Pater Noster' mille ducenta legunt.
O si papa forem uel patrum maximus abbas    f. 167r [olim 166r]
    Donec pro uiuis ius ita pingue darem!
Quippe recenseri fratrum michi nomina uellem
    Hic ego, quos vrsi commoluere truces,
485 Qui liuore patrum consumpti terga dedere,
    Ne fierent typicis pastus et esca lupis.
Talibus afflictis lacrimas, ieiunia, psalmos,
    Missarum cantus, thura, precesque darem.
Denique plus esset pro uiuis sumere planctum
490    Quam pro defunctis, quos loca pacis habent.
Ultima debetur defunctis gratia tandem,
    Res est pro uiuis semper agenda prior.

**Zelator:**

Qui mores hominum uitamque redarguit omnem
    Sole magis clarus plus niue mundus erit,
495 Huius pollute iam non erit incola terre,
    Ymmo poli ciuis uel, paradise, tuus.

---

469] om Me | 470 pecus] gregem Co, Me | 471 liuore] amore Gh | 471–73] om Me | 475 Multa statuta parent] Addunt et alia Me, parant Ot | 478] om Me | 480 legunt] ponunt Me | 482 Donec . . . ita] Potius . . . ego Me | 483–87] om Me | 487 lacrimas] lacrimis Co | 489–90] om Me | 490] Me substitutes l. 486 | 491–92] om Me | 494 clarus] clare Co | 495 pollute] impollute Co, iam om Me

snake cutting itself into three pestilential parts, if such a thing is allowed, smears everything there is in the world. But Lot escaped the curse of Sodom, (500) David the corruption of Pride, Joseph the monster of Envy. Once you were a cedar, you exceeded all the glory of the forest, now you lie flat like a bit of heather beneath the feet of the brothers. Let it be the case that something, I know not what, offends you in this matter. There is no great good man but he would prefer to be less. From the gospel we know this doctrine, that anyone who wants to be the boss will be the servant. But as I see it, that old antithesis is not yet laid to rest, the greater struggle still continues. And anyway, who would be less?

Do you know the fable of the king of the forest? (510) The woods went to seek a king for themselves. The votes were first the fig tree, then the vine, then the olive, and the three spoke as one, 'Take the kingship away from us!' Those noble trees shun the burden, but the shameless bramble asks for the sceptre, proclaiming: 'Let every grove of trees be a citizen!' The bramble still rules throughout all the cloisters, for there was scarcely anyone who would want to be nothing. Everyone seeks some higher place, everyone anticipates great things for himself. One of them grabs an ecclesiastical office, another an estate, yet another is the prince's favourite. Arise! Yield to Drusus! (520) You wretches whose origin was the cedar, behold! the audacious Hannibal, enormous of body, arrives with force. You trembling mice, get ready to flee. This new Cicero has a very sharp wit; you witless men defend yourselves!

---

**499–500** For Lot and Sodom Gen 19:15-25; for Joseph Gen 49 and 50; for David I Reg 25:32-35 and 26:9-11. | **501** Cf. l. 435 above. | **504** Cf. LSSM, p. 75, no. 28. **505–06** Matth 20:26 and 23:11; Marc 10:43. | **509–16** Iud 9:8–16. Cf. Odo of Cerinton, "Fabulae," FL, IV, pp. 175–77, 319–20, 335, and 423. See also J. Klapper, *Exempla aus Handschriften des Mittelalters* (Heidelberg, 1911), p. 76. The point of the story is not the democratic declaration at 514 but rather the recognition of ambition in 516. | **519–21** Drusus and Hannibal figure in Horace, *Carmina*, 4, 4, 18 and 49, where Drusus' victory over the Vindelici is celebrated. | **523** Tullius = M. T. Cicero.

Tres in pestiferas se scindens uipera partes
    Tale licet maculet omne quod orbis habet—
Loth tamen euadit Sodome contagia, Dauid
500    Fermentum fastus, inuida monstra Ioseph.
Olim cedrus eras nemoris decus omne preibas,     f. 167v
    Sub pede nunc fratrum prona myrica iaces.
Esto quid offense tibi nescio fiat in hac re—
    Nemo bonus maior sed studet esse minor.
505 Ex euangelio doctrinam nouimus istam,
    Quod qui uult maior esse minister erit.
Sed uetus, ut uideo, nondum contencio dormit,
    Durat adhuc maior. Quis sit itemque minor?
Scisne parabolicam nemorum de rege fabellam?
510    Iuerunt regem querere ligna sibi.
Uota fuerunt prima ficulnea, uitis, oliua,
    E tribus imperium tollat ut vna sibi.
Styps sacra uitat onus, sceptrum petit improba rampnus,
    Pontificat rampnus: 'Sit ciuis omne nemus.'
515 Regnat adhuc eadem per claustra per omnia rampnus
    Nam uix est aliquis qui nichil esse uelit.
Alta petunt omnes, presumunt grandia cuncti.
    Hic personatum preripit, ille locum,
Principis iste nepos est. Surgite! Cedite Druso!
520    Uos miseri, quorum cedrus origo fuit,
Hannibal ecce uenit vi uasti corporis, audax.     f. 168r [olim 167r]
    Uos pauidi mures, anticipate fugam.
Tullius iste nouus multo sale proluit ora;
    Uos salis expertis ore tenete uiri.

---

497–500] om Me | 497 pestiferas] pestiferos Gh | 503 om Me, re] rei Co | 506 line 516 inserted after 506 Me | 507–08] om Me | 510 iuerunt] Inierant Me | 511 fuerunt] Uocauerunt Co | 513 Styps] Strips Gh, Stirps Me, Ot, onus . . . rampnus] eius . . . ramnis Me | 515 per] proh Ot | 519 principis] princeps Co, Druso] Truso Me | 521] om Me | 523–24] om Me | 523 proluit] colluit Co | 524 expertis] extorres Co

Here's a trivial little story: a fairly serious argument over one's place in the hierarchy broke out among some monks. Little by little in some way or another things got worse—often a small spark causes huge fires. People arrived, here and there friends and relatives brought weapons; (530) one faction installed its monk at the top. This was already a long-standing quarrel. Finally one of the wise briefly spoke thus: 'What sort of a quarrel is this among monks for positions of authority as long as there is food fit for men? That order and that position seem to me best in which each is respected for his own part: those who serve in the kitchen, those who serve as monks, those who serve as priests.' Those who celebrate mass as a drunken orgy will produce weapons on the slightest pretext, such as positions in the hierarchy. The order is full of such types, (540) and they, being a law unto themselves, observe no laws. There is no place for humble men; humble men serve their convent, but this lot loves night's revelries. Oh how often have I seen monks meeting with monks the morning after—believe me. Some came to put a gloss on the night's celebrations, others to find a comfortable bed for their hungover bodies. What pain is it then, what fellow-feeling breaks you, if now and then they run off—those who are fleeing from their own guilt. Straw cannot withstand the force of the wind, (550) the flame that purifies gold will destroy the shrubbery. The sea casts up drowned bodies on the shores, but it sustains those in whom there is any breath. The sharp-beaked stork pushes its weak chick out of the nest, but cherishes in the nest the one who is strong enough.

---

547–70 An extended set of instances illustrating where a part is excised for the good of the whole.

|525| Accipe ridiculum: monachos contentio quosdam
Acrior inuasit pro statione loci.
Quolibet ex modico paulatim maxima surgunt—
Sepe dat eximios parua fauilla rogos.
Arma mouent, ciues ueniunt, hinc inde parentes;
|530| Installat monachum pars utraque in arce suum.
Certatum per longa fuit iam tempora; tandem
Unus prudentum sic ait ore breui:
'Que lis pro monachis vel eorum sedibus altis,
Dummodo non desint prandia lauta uiris?
|535| Optimus ille michi status esse uidetur et ordo
In quo par cunctis: olla, cuculla, calix.'
Pro leuibus causis, puta sedibus, arma mouebunt
Orgia qui celebrant ebria festa Dei.
Talibus a cephalis est ordo plenus, et isti,
|540| Lex sibimet facti, nulla statuta tenent.
His cum simplicibus non est pars ulla; minores     f. 168v
Conuentum seruant, hij meta noctis amant.
O quotiens monachos monachis occurrere uidi
In matutino tempore, crede michi.
|545| Hij nocturnales ueniebant soluere laudes,
Hij lassata mero membra locare thoro.
Quis dolor est igitur, que te compassio frangit,
Si passim fugiant quos sua culpa fugat?
Non potuerunt palee uim uenti sustimuisse,
|550| Aurum que purgat flamma frutecta uorat.
Proicit ad litus extincta cadauera pontus,
Sustinet illa quibus spiritus ullus inest.
Proicit infirmum rostrata cyconia pullum,
Confouet hunc nido qui ualuisse potest.

---

527–28] om **Me** | 530 utraque] utra **Ot** | 531 longa] multa **Co** | 535 michi status] status michi **Co** | 538 Orgia] Jurgia **Me** | 539–40 om **Me** | 547 te compassio] te et compassio **Me** | 548 sua culpa] deus ipse **Me** | 549 uim uenti sustinuisse] ventos et flamina ferre **Co, Me** | 550] om **Me** | 552 spiritus ullus inest] est aliquisque calor **Co, Me** | 554] om **Me**

Setting rank aside, why do some monks leave their cloister? It's an old and yet a pertinent question, none more so. The heavenly angel drove Adam out of Paradise; Judas the traitor left the group of apostles. Nicholas the Apostate would not accept his chosen destiny. (560) Many people have abandoned their first faith. Neither an austere abbot nor a stern order always prevents the return of villains behind their backs. Dukes sometimes decline and do not conform to their lineage. Nero himself finally became debauched. Flowers do not always produce viable seeds; those which the winds do not blow away may bear fruit. Not every vat of grapes crushed at the press produces good wine; dregs are acceptable for swine but only pure stuff for the gods. When a warrior straps on his weapons, no one knows who may carry off the prize of victory or (570) who may succumb. There is a God in whose hands our ends are shaped, who regulates and controls the fates of men.

You blame the law of the abbots and the general rule, in which our glory always consists. But I think that neither peace nor love can dwell among us if it were not for the sacred regulations. Just as the reins and the bridle control a team, so the fitting regulations of the fathers unite us. And what if the shepherd does not observe everything to the letter, (580) will the flock then be completely free of control? Huge whales cannot be taken with nets, but the other lesser school is netted onto the deck. So not every sort of law will bind our superiors, but underlings should be able to bear everything. What crime is it then if better food is prepared for those on whom falls the responsible care of the flock? By no means do

---

557 Gen 3:23. | 558 Matth 27:5. | 559 Probably Nicholas of Antioch, mentioned as a disciple in Act 6:5; his sect the Nicholaites condemned in Apoc 2:6 and 14-15. See also DTC XI, col. 499–506. | 564 Among the multitude of excesses of which Suetonius accuses Nero, gluttony is only casually alluded to in 6, 27 (... dispositae per litora et ripas deversoriae tabernae ...) and 6, 51 (... ventre proiecto ...). Tacitus, *Annales* 12-18 says nothing of his eating habits. | 567 molle Calenum, vintage wine from Cales (modern Calvi, Campania). Cf. Horace, *Carmina*, 1, 20, 9, and Juvenal, 1, 69. | 571 This line foreshadows Hamlet's "There is a divinity that shapes our ends"

| 555 | Ordine postposito, cur fratres claustra relinquunt?
|     |     Est uetus atque rudis questio, nulla magis.

555     Ordine postposito, cur fratres claustra relinquunt?
        Est uetus atque rudis questio, nulla magis.
    Angelus e celo ruit Adam de paradyso,
        Liquit apostolicum traditor ille chorum.
    Non tulit electam Nycolaus apostata sortem,
560         Innumeri primam deseruere fidem.
    Non pater austerus rigidus nec semper id ordo   f. 169r [olim 168r]
        Efficit ut redeant post sua terga mali.
    Degenerant quandoque duces, nec stema sequuntur:
        Ipse Nero tandem ganeo factus erat.
565     Non semper flores veniunt ad germinis usum,
        Fructificant quos non uentus et aura tulit.
    Efficitur mustum non totum molle Calenum;
        Fex satiat porcos, limpida gutta deos.
    Nemo scit optatos quis portet ab hoste triumphos
570         Aut quis succumbat, dum pugil arma ligat.
    Est Deus in manibus cuius sunt tempora nostra,
        Qui sortes hominum temperat atque regit.
    Arguis abbatum ius et generale statutum
        In quo consistit gloria nostra simul.
575     Estimo nec pacem nec amorem posse morari
        Inter nos si non sacra statuta forent.
    Quomodo frena domant et dura lupata iugales,
        Sic nos componunt digna statuta patrum.
    Et quid si pastor non omnia seruat ad unguem,
580         An grex idcirco remige liber erit?
    Retibus includi non possunt grandia cete,   f. 169v
        Clauditur hijs ponti cetera turba minor.
    Sic neque prelatos quecumque statuta ligabunt,
        Subiecti debent omnia posse pati.

---

(V, ii, 10). The sentiment is common enough, but I find no earlier trace of this wording nor any connection between this line and Shakespeare.

---

**555** reliquunt] relinquant **Me** | **563** stema] stamma **Co** | **563–64**] om **Me** | **576** Inter nos] In claustro **Me** | **581–82**] om **Me**

priors prepare sumptuous banquets for themselves but rather for the poor and for their guests.

Now then, I shall put no further confidence in you nor believe you (590) unless you provide an example to prove these evil deeds. For who would believe you—that there may be among holy and faultless men such things as guile, violence, malice? I do not deny it myself, but unless you offer proof of these crimes, no cowl will cover this head again. Let disparagement stop because there is nothing believable. Wicked words corrupt good morals. The Egyptian Ammon hated the Hebrew shepherds but loved the tillers of the earth; so the mob hates the yoke of control.

**Persecutor:**

I had three abbots, apart from the one who first (600) girded me with the sash of celibacy. The one who first made me a monk was peaceful and easy going; he neither annoyed nor pleased me. I would prove that the three others were just like bears, except that they had no tails at their backsides. I also note this: that they did not live in the desert but in clean monasteries with food and luxurious beds. The worst of these three, under whom I left my cloister, is the example through whom my greatest accusations are clearly evident. Leaving me out for a bit, (610) let me show you something of the abbot's pernicious jealousy and powerful guile. Alas for me that I do not know how to flatter the sins of the gods, not even if Jupiter himself were to sin could I bear it. By God, I even said that such fearful things were the products of a deranged mind.

Here is a detestable crime I witnessed under this abbot. The odious abbot hated one of us, hated him and attacked him with manipulative

---

591 Cf. 469, above.  |  596 Cf. Walther, Prov, I, 3576, 3579, 3580; I Cor 15:33. 597–98 Ex 1:7–14 narrates how the vigorous health of the Hebrew slaves struck fear into the Egyptians. Hamon = Ammon.

| 585 | Quod scelus est igitur si pinguor olla paretur
| | Hijs quibus incumbit prouida cura gregis?
| | Nequaquam pro se conuiuia lauta priores
| | Sed pro pauperibus hospitibusque parant.
| | Iam tibi nec fides nec ero bene credulus ultra
| 590 | Exemplum nisi des quo mala facta probes.
| | Nam tibi quis credat—astus, uiolentia, liuor,
| | Quod sint in sanctis et sine labe uiris.
| | Ipse nec infitior: scelus hoc si forte probabis,
| | Hoc caput obnubet nulla cuculla magis.
| 595 | Quod quia possibile non est detractio cesset,
| | Corrumpunt mores uerba prophana bonos.
| | Oderat Egyptus Hammonis amore colendi
| | Pastores ouium, sic uaga turba iugum.

**Persecutor:**

| | Tres michi, preter eum qui primum celibe cultu
| 600 | Hec mea precinxit membra, fuere patres.
| | Primus erat placidus et blandis moribus aptus,<sup>f. 170r [olim 169r]</sup>
| | Qui me non turbat nec placet ille michi.
| | Tres alios vrso similes satis esse probarem,
| | A tergo nisi quod non sibi cauda fuit.
| 605 | Hoc eciam saluo quod non deserta colebant,
| | Sed loca lauta cibis zelotiposque thoros.
| | Pessimus iste trium, sub quo mea claustra reliqui,
| | Est instans per quod maxima nostra patent.
| | Me sine paulisper, quod te de pernice zelo
| 610 | Et patris expediam uique doloque simul.
| | Heu michi! Quod nequeo vicium palpare deorum,
| | Set neque si peccet Iupiter ipse feram.
| | O dolor! Et dixi capitis metuenda frenesis.
| | Accipe quod uidi sub patre triste scelus.

---

585–86] om Me | 589–94] om Me | 591 Nam] Iam; uiolencia Co | 594 obnubet] obnubes Co | 595 possibile] credendum Co, Me | 598 sic] odit Me, Me adds Sepe scolares cum virga aspera iustum | 599 Tres] res Gh | 601–06] om Me | 602 nec] nam Ot | 607 reliqui] relinquo Me | 608–68] om Me | 613 dixi] diri Gh, Ot

malice: 'On the shore of the sea there is a daughter house of our cloister, a subordinate house lying almost beneath the cold of Arcturus, where there are Ryphean winters with sharp grains of hail—(620) all this we see in your zodiac sign, burnt Cancer. There is no field of grain there nor the fat olive tree, nor does the elm woven with vines support any sweet grapes. Here is the altar of the goddess Tethios, Neptune's own corner exhales thicker clouds than the river Styx. The land is said to be where the earth swallowed Cere, an area of marshy sand which has on occasion buried the bodies of a thousand men. Here is the tongue of the sea which the sea god Nereus raises up through his open mouth over the inhabitants, as he takes away their lands. Conflict keeps some people under control, but the Sirtican territory, (630) against which they vainly consider resisting, controls this group. They have, however, certain superstitious restraints, which are effective when there is a half moon or a new moon; but if there is a full moon or a quarter moon, then everyone fears Deucalion's flood. Then both sexes and all ages cling together to a raft of floating logs, and every man flees to the towers. Many people hang like Zacheus hung from the top of a tree to see Jesus, bearing the gift of salvation. But when the

---

**617–58** The abbot's rhetoric very nearly gets the better of him, but remember that he wants to threaten the 'ex nobis quendam' (615) by describing a place, somewhere on the northern coast of Europe (?), a place of great cold and discomfort, even though not all the place names are clear. But cf. Ovid, *Ex Ponto*, I, 3, 65-82 for a similar catalogue of persons and places associated with cold and wet weather. | **619** Rypheas = CL Rhiphaeas, referring to a range of mountains said to be in the north. Mentioned by Statius, *Thebaid*, 1, 420; spicula grandinis, Alanus ab Insulis, *Anticlaudianus*, ed. R. Bossuat (Paris, 1955), 1, 70. | **620** Cancer is the fourth sign of the Zodiac, 20 June to 22 July. The abbot assumes that those under the sign of Cancer are unsuited to life in a cold climate. | **621** Ceres, goddess of corn and harvests, the mother of Proserpina, whose search for her daughter is narrated in Ovid, *Metam*, 5, 438–571. **623** Derived from Tethys, the sea; Neptunius, an adjective derived from Neptunus, the sea god | **624** The well-known river Styx in the underworld, mentioned, e.g., by Vergil, *Aeneid* 6, 317–30. | **625–26** The fate of Core is narrated in Num 16:1–35. He and several others rebelled against Moses and Aaron and were swallowed by the earth for their punishment. The phrase 'fata Core' also occurs in Theodulus, *Ecloga*, l. 153. See Teodulo, *Ecloga: il canto della verità e della mensogna*, ed. Francesco Mosetti Casaretto: Testi mediolatini con traduzione (Florence, 1997). | **627** Nereus, a sea god,

## Liber de duobus monachis

615 Oderat ex nobis quendam pater iste malignus,
    Oderat et tacita fraude petebat eum:
'Est quedam nostri supra mare filia claustri,
    Pene sub Ar<c>turi frigore cella latens,
Rypheas hyemes et spicula grandinis illic
620     Uidimus in signo, Cancer aduste, tuo.
Non ibi culta Ceres nec pinguis oliua nec ulmus     f. 170v
    Uitibus intexta dulce retentat onus.
Thecios ara dee, Neptunius angulus iste
    Exalat nebulas plus Stigis amne graues.
625 Tellus fata Chore, tellus stagnantis arene
    Obruit interdum corpora mille uirum.
Hec est lingua maris, toto quam Nereus ore
    Exerit in ciues, ut sua rura tulit.
Bella domant alios, istos loca Syrica ciues,
630     Contra quem uanum bella mouere putant.
Attamen hijs quedam sunt sancta repagula, que si
    Dycothomos fuerit uel noua luna, ualent,
At si Pansylenos uel sit modo ciclica Phebe,
    Tunc sibi quisque timet Deucalionis aquas.
635 Tunc trabibus celsis simul omnis sexus et etas
    Heret, et ad turres confugit omnis homo.
Plurimus hic summa tunc pendet ab arbore Zacheus

---

figures sporadically in Ovid, Metam, 2, 268; 11, 361; 12, 94; 13, 742. | ‡629 Syrtica, a stretch of shore along the Mediterranean coast of North Africa, including the present site of Leptis Magna in Libya. It was generally considered sandy, desert-like, barren. The abbot's geography is a little off, but his intent is evidently to terrify the monk he dislikes with a vision of a sea-bound coast lifted directly from North Africa to this unnamed northern place. | **632** dychotomos = dichotomos, halved or half moon. | **633** Pansylenus = panselenus, the full moon. | **634-44** Cf. Ovid, *Tristia* 1, 2, 14-36. | **637-38** Luc 19:2-4. Extra syllable in the fourth foot.

618 Ar<c>turi . . . latens] arturi; **Co, Gh, Ot**, acturi; . . . iacens **Co** | 621 ibi] tibi **Co** 626 uirum] uirorum **Co** | 627 Nereus] uterus **Co** | 628 Exerit erexit **Co** | 629 Syrica] Syrtica **Gh** | 630 quem] que **Co** | 633 ciclica Phebe] tydica plede **Co** | 637 Plurimus] Pluribus **Co**

time of the lethal flood is over, (640) then you'll wander through many sea monsters in the middle of the roads. I myself, protected by a shield and weapons, have seen that that terrifying bay was holding fish. And even though the turbulent ocean may surround the strong sea walls, there is nonetheless a deadly thirst for fresh water. A sailor approaches by ship, but if there is any delay and the sailor is swept away by the force of the sea—what do you think happens then? Then children and pregnant mothers and those burning with fever, however parched the shore may be, they rush to every available bit of beach. They shout with several voices to the slow-witted captain, (650) while filling the shore with disorderly cries. Often they call to the sailor, for the sound of one's own name is sweeter than the names of one's mother or father. Then a thirsty flock of birds is borne through the clouds calling out and seeking everywhere the missing sailor. When this captain has at last been found by chance, they beg for water barrels, revealing their thirst with gestures and signs. Then rejoicing they clamber up the water barrel, scratch it with their weakened claws. They ask for water for everyone, and he knows how to get it.'

If this ferocious expeller wanted to punish anyone, (660) he exiled or imprisoned him. And the latest suspect, however innocent he may have been before, from the time he came here he was always suspect. There are monasteries that do not know how to get rid of a criminal, and there are containers in which no washing has any effect. A girl playing outside a brothel is suspect, just as she is if she has entered only to chase a ball. Such suspicion should not seem trivial to you, for sometimes suspicion

---

**643** Cf. Ion 2:6. | **644** Cf. Ovid *Ex ponto* 3, 1, 17–18. | **643–58** The final bits of the abbot's speech of terror. I think the magister and the nauta are the same person. The people all run to the shore to beg water from the nauta. The cohors of 653 is the antecedent of the singular verbs in 654–58, but my translation takes the birds as the antecedent on the grounds that they are the logical antecedent. | **645–52** Cf. Ovid *Tristia* 1, 11, 21–22. | **661** i.e., the man the abbot detested, first mentioned at l. 615. **664** Cf. LSSM p. 34, no. 86.

Ut uideat Iesum, ferre salutis opem.
Ast ubi letiferi pertransijt hora lauacri,
640     Multa leges medijs monstra marina uijs.
Uidi ego, qui fuerat clipeo protectus et armis,   f. 171r [olim 170r]
    Piscem terribiles hos tenuisse sinus.
At licet in gyro fera menia uallet abissus,
    Hic uiui laticis est tamen atra sitis.
645 Classibus aduehitur, quod si quandoque moratur,
    Ui maris abreptus nauta quid esse putas?
Tunc pueri tunc grauide matres et febribus usti,
    Quamuis litus arent, litus ad omne ruunt.
Compellunt tardum vario clamore magistrum
650     Confusaque simul litora uoce replent.
Sepe uocant nautam, nam uox sibi nomine huius
    Dulcior est matrum nominibusque patrum.
Tunc uolucrum sitibunda cohors per nubila clamans
    Fertur, et amissum querit ubique uirum.
655 Supplicat, inuento tandem fortasse magistro,
    Gestibus imponens indicijsque sitim,
Dolia. Scandit ouans tenero fricat vngue lagenas,
    Poscit aquas cunctis, scit quibus ille modis.'
Huc ferus exactor, si quem punire uolebat,
660     Misit in exilium carceribusque dabat.
Is quoque suspectus, clarus licet ante fuisset,   f. 171v
    Qui semel huc uenit, a modo semper erat.
Sunt loca que sceleris nequeunt abolere reatum,
    Et sunt uasa quibus lotio nulla ualet.
665 En suspecta redit que luserat ante lupanar,
    Si semel intrauit uirgo secuta pilam.
Nec tibi suspicio debet res parua uideri,

---

640 Multa ... monstra] Monstra ... multa Co | 647 Tunc ... tunc] Tunc ... et Co | 653 uolucrum], ... cohors] auium ... choris Co | 656 imponens] exponens Ot 657 fricat ... lagenas] tenera, secus ... lagenam Co | 658 ille] illa Ot | 659 Huc] Hunc Co | 660 Misit] dedit Co | 665 En] Et Co

attaches to the place of the crime. Suspicion is like Lamech's misdirected arrow, (670) which killed a man he thought was an animal. Even the prophet Heli in the dim light believed that Anna was drunk. And Judas, not realizing that it was his beloved daughter-in-law, asked Tamar, who was waiting at the crossroads, to play the harlot. So sometimes the harsh presumption of the abbots considers us guilty and presses their false suspicions upon us. Our brother suffered to the greatest extent the loss of his reputation, and the exile imposed on him, and the penalty of shame. The matter was out of our hands, for this psychopathic tyrant (680) ordered our suspected brother to leave. The accused dreaded the place, the public damage to his reputation, the cold of the snow, the turbulence of the sea.

The opinion of the abbots always has a great deal of authority and very little sense of compassion. Israel will be unconquered so that Ioab may take the census, but David was himself broken by his own power. Neither a doe nor a ewe fights off fierce tigers, nor does a dove resist a hawk for very long. Our brother was exiled—but what is more lamentable, (690) he went to his death at the command of this merciless abbot.

Not only that, the prior here was worse than Busirus and crueller than the savage Phalaris. When he heard that a guest was coming, this

---

**669-70** Gen 4:23–24. Cf. Bede, *Hexaemeron* PL 91: 76. | **671–72** I Reg 1:13–16. For Heli's blindness see I Reg 3:2 and 4:15. | **673–74** Thais, a noted hetaera said to have been Alexander the Great's mistress, is mentioned in Ovid, *Ars amatoria* 3, 604 and *Remedia amoris* 383 ff. The poet here uses her name figuratively in reference to Gen 38:14–19. | **685** II Reg 24:1–12. | **686** David's death is narrated in III Reg 1–2:1-10. | **689** The subject of Itur is the same unfortunate we first met in 615. | **691–92** Ovid, *Metamorphosis* 9, 182–83, tells how Hercules, in his quest to steal the cattle of Geryon, kills Busiris the Egyptian tyrant, reputed to sacrifice strangers who came to his court. In the *Ars amatoria* 1, 651–54, Ovid mentions both Busiris and Phalaris, the tyrant of Agrigentum, who roasted his victims in a bronze bull. | **693** Cerberus,

Obtinet interdum criminis illa locum.
Suspicio deforme Lamechque sagitta est,
670 Que feriens hominem credidit esse feram.
Lampadis extincte speculator et agnitor Hely
Annam crediderat ebrietate premi.
In biuio positam petijt pro Thaide Thamar
Iudas, ignorans quod foret alma nurus.
675 Sic quandoque reos patrum presumptio seua
Nos facit et falsa suspitione petit.
Plurimus hinc frater patitur dispendia fame,
Sustinet exilium, dampna pudoris habet.
Res est pre manibus, nam turbidus iste tyrannus
680 Hunc sibi suspectum compulit ire uirum.
Horruit ille locum causatus, publica fame   <sup>f. 172r [olim 171r]</sup>
Detrimenta, niuis frigora, vimque freti.
Preualet in cunctis semper sententia patrum
Multa potestatis pauca salutis habens.
685 Israel ut numeret Ioab inuictissimus exit,
Imperio Dauid frangitur ipse tamen.
Tygribus indomitis nec cerua nec agna repugnant,
Obstat et accipitri nulla columba diu.
Itur in exilium—sed quod lacrimabile plus est,
690 Itur ad interitum patre iubente fero.
Hoc neque preteream—prior hic Busiride peior
Atque fero Phaliri toruior unus erat.
Hospitis aduentum prenoscens, Cerberus iste

---

the three-headed guard dog of Hades, is mentioned in Vergil, *Aeneid* 6, 417–18; Ovid, *Metamorphosis* 4, 450 and 7, 413. | **693–702** Hostility toward a guest flouts all the recommendations in *Reg mon*, cap. 53, "De hospitibus suscipiendis."

669 Sagitta] sagratas **Gh** | 670 Que] qui **Me**, quo **Ot** | 671–74] om **Me** | 675 presumptio] suspicio **Me** | 676 facit . . . petit] putat . . . premit **Co**, portat . . . premit **Me** | 677 Plurimus hinc] hunc **Co**, Plurima **Me** | 679 iste] ille **Me** | 680 Hunc] Huc **Gh** | 682] om **Me** | 685–87] om **Me** | 685 exit] erit **Co** | 691-2] om **Me** | 693 Cerberus iste] Terberus, alter **Me**

Cerberus met him and harassed him even at the outside gate. 'Tell me,' he said, 'if you have a sorry record of some odious sin. Open up your purse. Let it be emptied. Let it be emptied right here in our midst, for you will not be allowed anything to eat until a list of your sins is made known. You will not deceive me the way an earlier visitor recently did: (700) he ate his meal and ran off—without providing a list of his sins. I don't know what traitor might have tipped him off so that the chosen victim escaped my knife.' As our guest heard this, he turned his eyes hither and thither but found no path that offered him escape. For at some distance a boat damaged by the sea was moored, and from the summit of the rocks there was eternal chaos—for that was the place, fearful Scylla, where the panther Charybdis mingled herself with your whirlpools. So he produced his writings sealed with pitch (710) such as Uriah carried to his fate. Reading the text the tormentor smiled nicely and said, 'Don't you know why you were sent here as a victim? You must know, unless perhaps because you are not in chains here nor is there any sign of torture. Aren't your secret poisons and plague rightly revealed by the pepper sauce of an old abbot?'

That was the end of the speech, and our guest did not postpone his death; in a brief moment he ended a long wait—he threw himself precipitately into the sea, saying, 'Take me, (720) take wretched me, brief Scylla, from a long prison sentence.' Believe me, with my own astonished eyes, I myself saw the place, the leap, the deep sea of the turbulent pit.

---

706 Chaos derives from many sources, but cf. Ovid, *Metamorphoses*, 1, 7. | **707–08** Ovid, *Metamorphoses*, 13, 730–32. Usually characterised as a monstrous female, Charybdis seems here to have become a panther, from an unknown source. | **710** II Reg 11:14–15, where David sends Urias to his certain death in order to have access to

|     | Obuiat et primo limine turbat eum. |
| --- | --- |
| 695 | 'Dic,' ait, 'inuisi sceleris si pagina tristis |
|     | Est tibi. Fac loculo prodeat ille suo. |
|     | Prodeat in medium, nec enim prandere licebit |
|     | Donec nequitie sit nota lecta tue. |
|     | Non me decipies, uelud is qui prandia nuper |
| 700 | Sumpsit et effugit—nec sua scripta dedit. |
|     | Nescio quis uigilem sibi proditor imbuit aurem, |
|     | Ut fugeret cultros uictima missa meos.' |
|     | Hospes, ut audiuit, oculos hinc inde reflexit, |
|     | Nec tamen inuenit qua fuga ferret iter. |
| 705 | Nam procul auulsa reduci stetit equore cimba, |
|     | Et fuit a summa rupe perenne chaos— |
|     | Nam locus iste fuit qua se panthera Caribdis |
|     | Miscet porticibus, Scilla timenda, tuis. |
|     | Ergo sigillatas profert de pixide cartas, |
| 710 | Urias quales in sua fata tulit. |
|     | Scripta legens tortor lepide subrisit et inquit, |
|     | 'An nescis quare uictima missus ades? |
|     | Immo scies, nisi forte loco sua vincula desint |
|     | Et tormentorum dormiat omne genus. |
| 715 | Nonne lues merito submissa uenena latentur |
|     | In piper abbatis iussidulumque senis?' |
|     | Finis erat dictis, nec mortem distulit hospes, |
|     | Abstulit in puncto tedia longa breui— |
|     | In mare precipitem sese dedit. 'Accipe,' dixit, |
| 720 | 'Me miserum e longo carcere, Scilla breuis.' |
|     | Ipse locum, saltus, baratrique rotantis abyssum |

f. 172v (at line 701)
f. 173r [olim 172r] (at line 721)

---

Urias' wife, Bethsabee.  |  712 Cf. l. 702 where uictima is feminine, but here it is masculine in order to avoid elision with ades.

---

694 primo . . . limine] lumine **Gh**, eum turbat **Co**, sermo **Me**  |  695–702] om **Me**  702 missa] messa **Co** | 707–08] om **Me** | 708 porticibus] uerticibus **Co** | 711 Scripta] Scriptor **Me**  |  714–16] om **Me**  |  716 senis] semis **Gh**  |  721–34] om **Me**  |  721 rotantis] sonantis **Co**

For in fact I had at that time been sent away to those places and suffered much sorrow well beyond my guilt.

Happy is the man who suffers what his fault deserves, who understands for what sin he is being punished! Here I was considered both despised and suspect, for my monastic hood had been cut off. My clothing right down to the buttocks hung in tattered shreds, (730) and David, I was like your men whom Ammon shaved. Before the gates of the cloister I sat on the bare earth, and my meals were outside the temple with the dogs. No reverence was paid to this priest of Christ, violent hands dragged me away and beat me. Papal authority could not defend me—neither the power of a mandate nor a papal bull. To appeal against a judgement was both a crime and my most recent error—no voice was less audible to my tormentor. 'Woe unto you, you will be received by prison chains,' he said. (740) Do you know that an appellant is a curse in this place? As Rome holds the pope, so a prison will hold you, and a papal bull cannot help you now. Anyone may contribute some yellow gold for your sake, you don't suppose you will be exonerated for such a measly price? Let the pope order, let him order ten times and order again, this sacred institution will reject such swollen threats. Let him send thousands of documents authenticated with leaden seals—this is just what we ask for because the monastery needs metal. We can use a bull from the excited Thunderer: (750) the lead will make lamps and the rope it's attached with will make wicks. The parchment leaves will go to various uses—untanned it will make a collar round your neck, roasted it will be sticky tar.' With the monks then, in whose midst both guile and power lie

---

725–26 Cf. Ovid, *Tristia*, 1, 2, 95–100. | 730 II Reg 10:4. | 736, 742, 747 Papal bulls usually carried a lead seal (bulla) attached to the parchment by a cord of some sort, often a bit of rope. The ends of the rope were usually unravelled to give purchase to the wax seal on the parchment and the lead of the seal itself.

---

727 despectus . . . suspectus] suspectus . . . despectus **Co** | 731 resedi] sedi **Co** | 734 impegit] impingit **Co** | 735 me] enim **Me** | 736 Nec . . . nec . . . uiri] Non . . . non . . . viri **Me, Ot** | 738–40] om **Me** | 738 erat fuit **Co** | 740 appellans] appellas **Co** | 741 te] ter **Me** | 742–44] om **Me** | 743 quisquam] quicquam **Gh Co** | 744 num] non **Ot**

*Liber de duobus monachis*

Attonito uidi lumine, crede michi.
Nempe relegatus fueram tunc sedibus illis,
   Et preter culpam tristia multa tuli.
725 Felix qui patitur id quod sua culpa meretur,
   Qui nouit pro quo crimine uulnus habet!
Hic ego despectus simul et suspectus habebar,
   Nam precisa michi sacra cuculla fuit.
Uestis ad usque nates male detruncata pependit,
730    Parque fui, Dauid, hijs quos tibi rasit Amon.
Ante fores claustri nuda tellure resedi,
   Et michi cum canibus mensa prophana fuit.
Nulla sacerdoti facta est reuerentia Christi,
   Traxit et impegit me uiolenta manus.
735 Non me papalis poterat defendere uirtus,
   Nec uis mandati nec sacra bulla iuri.
Appellare fuit scelus et nouissimus error,
   Tortori nulla uox erat egra magis.
'Ue tibi carcereis,' ait, 'excipiende catenis,
740    Scisne quod appellans est anathema loco?
Cum papam sua Roma tenet, te carcer habebit,     f. 173v
   Nec poterit plumbi massa ualere tibi.
Conferret fuluum quisquam tibi forsitan aurum,
   Hoc precio uili num redimendus eris?
745 Mandet apostolicus, mandet deciesque remandet,
   Excludet tumidas hec sacra cella minas.
Mittat bullatas per mille uolumina cartas,
   Hoc est quod petimus—nam caret ere locus.
Utilis est nobis commoti bulla tonantis:
750    Urceolos plumbum—ligmina zona dabit,
Membrane series diuersos cedet in usus—
   Cruda collum cingit, cocta bitumen erit.'
Cum monachis igitur michique conuencio liuor,

---

745 Mandet] Mandat [for first mandet]Me | 746–49] om Me | 748 nam caret] indiget **Co** | 750 ligmena] licinina **Co** | 751 series] senes **Me**; **Me** conflates 751 with 752: Membrane senes torta bitumine erit | 752–56] om **Me**

hidden, envy was my indictment. The dying patriarch Jacob left Egypt, Joseph moved his bones from an unsuitable place. I am much afraid to tell you even worse things, for you are perhaps a novice. 'Even worse things'—for there are still two abbots to go (760) whose savagery no text could capture.

**Zelator:**

Since every master, every sacred supervisor, every good abbot is set up like a target, it's not surprising if one of them is wounded by a perverse arrow. Many malicious people lay traps for their superiors, and sometimes they prevail over the good ones. Why did Jerome, driven by his monks, leave Rome? He had written a book of their misdeeds. Why did your monks, Benedict, give you poison? (770) You derived a holy rule from their lives. Those who transport stones and those who cut wood will feel pain and will often be wounded. We are the stones and the wood out of which the house is to be built, a house with a celestial hall, worthy of God. Take a look at the methods of the builders, get to know their work, note the skill with which a worker brings his work to perfection. Perhaps the stones are rough or the wood warped, the cement weak, the bricks not properly baked in the oven. Cracked roof tiles will not keep out the rain (780) which will soak the rough beams and the fastenings will hang loose and twisted. And so a builder makes himself ready with all his skills, concentrating on his work because of the importance of the job. He sets about the stones and with firm chiselling shapes them, cutting away the bits he sees are unsuitable. He puts the finishing touches on the warped

---

755 Gen 49:30–31. | 756 Gen 50:25; Exod 13:19. | 767 AASS Sept. VIII, 476–80, tells how Jerome left Rome. The liber nequitie might have been his *Liber adversus Helvidium de virginitate Mariae perpetua* or perhaps his *Epistola ad Eustocium*, both of which take an extreme position on clerical celibacy. | 769 Greg II, iii, pp. 80–81, tells how Benedict's monks tried to poison him. (Also in PL 66: 135). | **771–806** This striking bit of imagery of building and building materials is apparently unique to this poem.

---

759–60] om Me | 760 nequitiam] seuitiam **Co**, **Me** adds l. 839 | 763 Quod] Quid

In quorum medio uisque dolusque latent.
755 Egiptum moriens Iacob patriarcha reliquit,
    Ossa Ioseph spurco sunt releuata loco.
Plura reformido, quia forte nouicius es tu,
    Enarrare tibi deteriora satis.
'Deteriora satis'—patres duo namque supersunt
760     Quorum nequitiam biblia nulla capit.

**Zelator:**                                                                           f. 174r [olim 173r]
Cum uelud ad signum positi sint quique magistri,
    Rectores sancti, prepositique boni,
Quid mirum prauo refert si uulnus ab arcu—
    Sicque notentur ab hijs quos nota multa notat.
765 Patribus insidias multi posuere maligni,
    Et quandoque bonis preualuere uiris.
Jeronimus Roma monachis cur pulsus abibat,
    Librum nequitie scripserat ille sue.
Cur monachi, Benedicte, tibi posuere uenenum,
770     De uita illorum regula sacra tibi est.
Qui transfert lapides et scindit ligna dolorem
    Sentiet et crebro uulnere lesus erit.
Nos lapides et ligna sumus, domus vnde struenda est,
    Aule celestis mansio digna Deo.
775 Aspice fabriles ritus, cognosce laborem,
    Cerne modum studij quo faber urget opus.
Sunt lapides fortasse rudes, sunt ligna recurua,
    Debile cementum, crudus ab igne later.
Tegula percussa pluuie non sustinet ymbres,
780     Hispida tigna rigent, lora repanda iacent.
Hinc igitur totis sc uiribus apparat auctor,    f. 174v
    Incumbens operi pro grauitate rei.
Aggreditur lapides et duris ictibus illos

---

Ot, refert] referat Me | 764 notentur] uocentur Co | 766 uiris] mali **Co, Me** | 770 sacra] sancta; **Co,** om **Me** | 775–76] om **Me** | 775 Aspice] inspice **Co** | 777 sunt] (2ⁿᵈ)] et **Me** | 778–80] om **Me** | 779 percussa] pertusa **Co,** ymbres] imbrem **Ot** | 781 auctor] actor **Gh** | 782 grauitate] grauidate; **Co,** om **Me**

wood, strengthens the weak cement, bakes again in the fire the half-baked bricks. He decorates the unadorned beams, he scrapes and smooths the rough timbers, he allows no cracks in the roof tiles. But even though he arranges everything in the right order, (790) even though he makes things round and turns them in a lathe and shapes the work, sometimes a stone, struck by a heavy mallet, will give off chips which may bruise his legs. The wood, distorted by a rough knot, resists and fights against the saw and exhausts his hands. Weak cement, blown to bits by the fierceness of a storm, brings shame to the builder and destruction to the building site. The soft clay of a brick may may cause a builder to blush, and a broken tile may cut a worker's head. Often enormous stones have killed the masons (800) and may cause the entire project to collapse. I have seen builders crushed by collapsed vaulting and their buildings have become their tombs. Samson was killed by shaking the pillars he touched; Job's collapsing house crushed his children. So we should not always blame the builders—on the contrary, sometimes the materials bring along their own weaknesses. Let him who can count the stars tell how much effort and care falls upon abbots. I am in no doubt that those whose (810) lives become the target for attacks of the depraved are similar to martyrs. Sometimes a public rage for conflict drives people forth, other times a private dispute secretly afflicts them. We can see these matters quite clearly in David, who is usually taken as the Old Testament example of a Christian bishop: the public enemy Goliath rushed openly to his weapons, the powerful man threatened the weaker one with his strength. Absolon secretly plotted against his father, and Achitophel threw himself into the fray, by stirring up trickery. So there are those who provoke their

---

801 I am not sure of the subject of precipitavit, as my translation shows. | 803 Iud 16:25-30. | 804 Iob 1:19. | 813–16 I Reg 17:1-51, esp. 48–49.

784 explanans] expoliens **Co**, **Me** | 785] om **Me** | 786 lateres] lateras **Me**, ab] in **Co** 787–800] om **Me** | 789 disponat] disponit **Co** | 791 circinet] curinet **Gh** | 791 dolabr\<a\>] dolaru **Gh**, **Ot**, dolabri **Co** | 792 crura] torua **Co** | 794 conterebrantque] conterebantque **Co** | 798 rupta] scissa **Co** | 802–04] om **Me** | 805 fabros . .

        Corripit, explanans quos uidet esse rudes.
785  Ligna recurua polit, cementum debile firmat,
        Inualidos lateres rursus ab igne coquit.
        Absque decore trabes exornat, et hispida tigna
        Radit et explanat, tegula nulla crepat.
        Sed quamuis recto disponat in ordine cuncta,
790    Circinet et tornet atque figuret opus,
        Saxa tamen quandoque graui concussa dolabr\<a\>
        Eiciunt crustas, que sua crura terant.
        Ligna reluctantur scabroso uertice curua,
        Despiciunt serram conterebrantque manus.
795  Debile cementum vi tempestatis abactum
        Fit pudor artifici discidiumque loci.
        Molle lutum lateris contaminat ora magistri,
        Et fecit artificis tegula rupta caput.
        Sepe neci lathomos ingentia saxa dedere,
800    Et super impositum precipitauit onus.
        Uidimus artifices rupta testudine pressos   f. 175r [olim 174r]
        Et sibi compositas esse sepulcra domos.
        Occubuit tactas Sanson quatiendo columpnas,
        Job sua contriuit pignora lapsa domus.
805  Non igitur fabros semper culpabimus, immo
        Ex se defectus res aliquando trahunt.
        Patribus immineat labor et solercia quanta
        Dicat qui stellas dinumerare potest.
        Martiribus similes illos nichil ambigo, quorum
810    Prauorum iaculis uita petenda datur.
        Publica nunc belli rabies foris impetit illos,
        Clancula nunc tacite lucta perurget eos.
        Possumus in Dauid manifestius ista uidere,
        Qui prelatorum gestat ubique typum:
815  Publicus ecce palam ruit hostis in arma Golias
        Exprobrat infirmum uiribus ille potens.

---

.culpabimus] culpabimus . . . semper **Me** | **806** defectus] defectum **Me** | **808** potest] ualet **Co** | **809** similes] simulans **Co, Me** | **812** clancula] Iacula; **Me, Co,** tacitu **Me**

superiors to quarrel publicly, (820) whom the greatest embellishment of aggression—namely cleverness, customs, eloquence, money, advice, force, attractiveness, appearance, family—assists. They give heed to nothing, not even to the power and authority of their superiors; they fail to see their own fate in slingshots and stones. There are even those who secretly set traps for their superiors and blacken the spotless indications of their good reputation with rumours. They insinuate something about others by repeated whispers; it lays the groundwork for trampling better qualified men underfoot.

But neither the one sinner nor the other goes unpunished, (830) but they reach a bad end fairly quickly. The order is opposed to such quarrelsome people whom not even a papal bull can help. The law is not usually the patron of error nor does justice often favour those who sin against themselves. Why men throw themselves headlong and hang themselves is something known only to God. This is the conclusion that the depths of the mind shrink from: they dread hell and both life and death strike them with fear. Without anyone forcing him Judas hurried to the noose—(840) criminal punishment put an end to his crime.

**Persecutor:**
Perhaps you hope one day to be an abbot and so you praise the malicious deeds of our superiors. If you know how to tolerate flaws, to put on a false face, to offer a sympathetic ear, then you will be the right man for an abbot. With such talent those for whom the glory of this world is slight

---

817–18 The full account of Absolom's plot against Saul is narrated in II Reg 15-18; Achitophel's gambit is described in 16:21–23. | 839–40 Matth 27:3–5.

---

817 conspirat] conspirans **Ot** | 818–24] om **Me** | 819 lacessunt] lavescunt **Ot**, lacescunt **Co** | 824 nec] non **Gh** | 826 Et maculant . . . signa] Denigrant . . . gesta

Absolon occulte conspirat prelia patri,
    Ingerit Achitophel se stimulante dolo.
Sunt ita qui patres in publica bella lacessunt,
820    Quos iuuat armorum maximus ille decor,
Scilicet ingenium, mores, facundia, census, ^(f. 175v)
    Consilium, uirtus, gratia, forma, genus.
Hij nichil attendunt uires et posse priorum,
    In funda et lapide nec sua fata uident.
825  Sunt et in occulto patribus qui scandala tendunt,
    Et maculant fame candida signa bone.
Instillant alijs per crebra susurria quidquid,
    Sufficit electos suppeditare uiros.
Non tamen impune grassabitur vnus et alter,
830    Sed referent finem sub breuitate malum.
Talibus oppositus est bellatoribus ordo,
    Hos neque papalis bulla iuuare solet.
Non solet errori lex esse patrona, nec ipsos
    In se qui peccat ius aliquando fouet.
835  Cur se precipitent homines laqueisque trucident
    Est tantum soli cognita causa Deo.
Hoc est iudicium quod mentis abhorret abyssus—
    Infera formidant uitaque morsque pauent.
Ad laqueum Judas nullo cogente cucurrit,
840    Imposuit sceleri pena scelesta modum.

**Persecutor:**
Abbatem speras te forsitan esse futurum     ^(f. 176r [olim 175r])
    Idcirco laudas impia facta patrum.
Si maculas inferre scias pretendere uultus,
    Tristes auriculas sugere dignus eris.
845  Hoc studio meruere thronos ascendere passim
    Hij quibus in mundo gloria parua fuit.

---

Me, bone] sua Co | 827–28] om Me | 833–34] om Me | 833 lex] nec Co | 834 peccat . . . fouet] peccant . . . fouent Co | 838–40] om Me | 838 formidant] formident Co | 839–955] om Co, because of the missing leaves; see Introduction., p. xxi | 843–50] om Me

generally deserve to ascend thrones. Thus such skill honoured, stinking labourers and those who perform menial duties. (850) Up to now a mere fuller who wants to be your and ipso facto the cloister's novice master attacks his groin repeatedly. Up to now any stranger armed with sword and weapons, a bold thief whom you embrace as your lord, a barber who may strike you in your prayers—do you fan his arse as he gives enemas? Now where does the law of Moses belch forth such scabby monsters of servants, bleary-eyed hunchbacks before God?

Here is a difficult situation for you—one which you could scarcely believe—I would like to tell you privately, and I beg you to be quiet about it. It's not customary in monasteries to punish any (860) misdeed more severely than the well-known clauses of the law, so I beg you to keep this to yourself.

There is a place where a single house not far from the monastery shelters five sisters. They mend, they take on duties—any practical needs of the brothers are given to them to be put in order in various ways. I gave them the job of repairing the fringe on the abbot's cloak, in order to prevent any ashes or dust from hurting his face, for he was bleary-eyed and couldn't see anything other than someone who sees the face of a gorgon in the mirror. At this point I don't want to tell you (870) which two brothers with stealthy steps rushed to this place. What do the wretches do? With the roof alone as witness, they entered the room and stole the cloak and also stole the girl's red-dyed clothing which hung on the same hook. They hid their loot in a hidey hole. Once these items were missed, there was a whisper in the cloister and serious anger from on high. The monastery, now divided into factions, withdraws, and each girl

---

847–56 The Persecutor testily criticises the limits of the Zelator's tolerance and willingness to forgive sin and sinners. | 855 The Law of Moses is expounded in Exod 20–23, with the Ten Commandments at 20:2–17. Needless to say no scabby monsters or bleary-eyed hunchbacks are mentioned. | 859–60 Reg Mon does not specify any particular punishments. | 868 Ovid, Metam 4, 782–85, tells of Perseus' seeing the Gorgon's snake-haired face reflected in his shield and thus avoids being turned to stone.

Cerdones olidos aut deteriora professos
    Officia hoc studium magnificauit ita.
Nudus adhuc fullo saltu querit inguina crebro
850    Qui tuus et claustri sic pedagogus erit.
Errat adhuc filius gladio precinctus et armis,
    Latro ferox dominum quem fateare tuum,
Sub nate uentolas et adhuc clisteria ponit?
    Tonsor qui pellet te statione tua?
855 Lex ubi nunc Moysi que scabida monstra ministri
    Lippos et gibbos nauseat ante deum?
Rem tibi difficilem, rem quam uix credere possis,
    Clam recitare uelim, teque tacere precor.
Non solet in claustro punire durius ullum
860    Crimen quam clausas ad fora ferre notas.
Vnde precor taceas. Locus est ubi quinque sorores    f. 176v
    Haut procul a claustro continet una domus,
Nent, et pensa trahunt, res fratrum quelibet illis
    In uarios usus expedienda datur.
865 Hijs curanda mee fuerat data fimbula cappe
    Ne cinis aut puluis lederet ora patris,
Lippus erat rector, alio nec lumine uidit
    Quam qui per speculum gorgonis ora tulit.
Huc se furtiuo gressu quos dicere nolo
870    E fratrum numero proripuere duo.
Quid faciunt miseri? Reserato lumine tecti
    Inuadunt cameram diripiuntque togam
Diripiunt etiam quod eodem uecte pependit
    Virginis induuium muricis arte rubrum.
875 Furta tegunt latebris. Fit murmur in edibus ipsis
    Desuper amissis rebus et ira grauis.

---

848 ita] ira **Gh** | 853 uentolas . . . clisteria ponit] uentosas **Ot**, coria stringit **Me** | 854 Tonsor] Torsor **Me** | 855–56] om **Me** | 856 gibbos] gibbosos **Ot** | 857 Rem] Nam **Me** | 863–908] om **Me** | 863 Nent . . . illis] Ad quas me transtuli vires ut recream meas **Me**

reports the other. Weeping they beat their breasts, and (880) by their own loss the wretched girls were ready to make good the other losses. That cloak required a loan; alas, she borrowed money with their cloaks as collateral.

The guilty brothers faked tears and the exhaustion of weeping. What's more they prepared a case to frame me. They went to the abbot and poured into that malicious father's ear whatever worthlessness fell from on high. I was summoned to a public meeting where there was a large crowd of men whom here favours and there fears of the abbot had influenced.

'Tell us, you wretch, where your heavenly clothing is now, (890) which a marriage of Venus stole from you? You shouldn't ask for sex at such a cost—love is often cheaper with just a little money.' Judas handed over the clasp of the cloak, and they asked the assembly, 'By the Bishop's crozier! Is this splendid clasp evidence against him? Does it not argue confinement? Often the brothers have told me of your disgraceful sins. Now this visible proof attests to your guilt without a witness. Now I know that you harassed these young girls and often laid hands on their chaste breasts. I have set things straight by what I have heard!'

His face withdrew along with his attitude. (900) I was dumbstruck. Finally after a long gap while I wanted to say something on my own behalf, that the witnesses have accused me of a crime. But they shouted, 'It is not fitting that this pestilential creature of the church should be heard, this man who, because of his unchaste behaviour, has caused this calamity. He is the very man who is known to have brought aggression against his own abbots and has deposed two of them. This mad man thinks he can depose our abbot—and he will do it!—unless he is guarded by our power!' The brothers constantly cry that I am worthy of prison, (910) and they order serious punishment as my fate.

Iam domus in partes a se diuisa recedit,
　　Iamque canet sociam queque puella suam
Pectora percutiunt flentes dampnoque cauere
880　　Netrices misere per sua dampna parant.
Obligat usuris hec pallia, proh dolor illa    f. 177r [olim 176r]
　　Mutuat in peplis (era minuta) suis.
Dissimulant fratres lacrimas et tedia flentum,
　　Arma parant fatis ulteriora meis.
885 Abbatem subeunt et quicquid stillat ab alto
　　Nequitie spargunt patris in aure feri.
Conuocor in medium series ubi densa uirorum
　　Quos patris immutat hinc timor inde fauor.
'Dicas, infelix, ubi nunc tua celica uestis
890　　Quam Ueneris thalami diripuere tibi.
Non tanta tibi luxus erat mercede petendus
　　Assibus exiguis sepe leuatur amor.'
Tradidit armillam Judas placitumque petunt
　　'Pro baculo! Est illi blanda patrata neruis?
895 Sepe mihi de te dixerunt turpia fratres,
　　Rem sine teste probat nunc oculata fides.
Nunc scio uestales te sollicitasse puellas
　　Inque sinus castos sepe tulisse manus.
Dirigui auditis.' Facies cum mente recessit.
900　　Pectore in attonito nec mihi sensus erat.
Tandem post longum dum pro me dicere uellem    f. 177v
　　Nequitie testes ostenuere meum ...
'Non debet,' clamant, 'audiri pestifer iste
　　Ecclesie qui res ob sua stupra dedit.
905 Hic est qui propriis abbatibus arma tulisse
　　Noscitur et patres deposuisse duos.
Estimat insanus quod et hunc deponere possit—
　　Et faciet—nostra ni tueatur ope.'
Clamant perpetuo me fratres carcere dignum

---

**882** era minuta] eraminura **Gh**

And that's how I fell, accused by the spite of my brothers. That's how the chaff assails the grain, how the weeds assail the roses. But yet there is no trickery without a judge before God who proves that affliction follows wicked men. For the first of them, paler than death, confessed his lies into the deaf ear of the choir master, while at the same time the other one, trumpeting louder than an elephant, started to be troubled by a devil.

Often in tears I went to the abbot and suppliant asked (920) that he would give me the protection of another cloister, for in fact I was afraid that those men might set new traps for me and plant wicked thefts in my room. That's how they were able secretly to spirit away my chalice and to put my neck in a frightful noose. My abbot concealed whatever he was planning against me—no one can satiate this man with my punishments. He wanted to put me on the coast of the Baltic Sea, far from the action, and that would be the end of the world, the Ultima Thule, for me. He had recently said that he wanted to send me to Syria—(930) I don't know why he delayed my journey through the Mediterranean. If there was peace among the great Assyrians or the Indians, then an Indian or an Assyrian would be my brother.

**Zelator:**
You report amazing things, but I would like to know what you were about to do that deserved overseas exile, which was not to a place of safety. Nor was it right for you to be punished nor yet to hear the cruel words of the old man—you were certainly not accustomed to the bliss of

---

914 secuta <esse> is the verb in indirect discourse—subject plaga, object infandos ... uiros. | 927 The Sarmatians were a Slavic tribe living between the Baltic and the Black Sea. Ovid uses the adjective frequently throughout the *Tristia* and the *Ex ponto* to evoke a cold and uncomfortable place. Valerius Flaccus also refers to the Sarmatians in his *Argonautica*, 8, 207 and 217. | 929–31 Syria, Assyrijs, Indis, Indus, Assyrius seem to refer generally to hot climates in the Middle East, in contrast to the Sarmaticas ... oras at 927.

## Liber de duobus monachis

910 Et dictant penas in mea fata graues.
Sic cecidi fratrum tactus liuore meorum,
   Sic granum palea pressit et alga rosam.
Attamen ante deum dolus est sine uindice nullus
   Qui probat infandos plaga secuta uiros,
915 Nam prior ex illis omni plus funere pallens
   Pertulit in surda canteris aure malum,
Alter demonio uexari cepit eodem
   Tempore barritu plus elephante fremens.
Sepe patrem lacrimis adij supplexque rogaui
920 Alterius claustri quod mihi septa daret,
   Nempe uiros timeo noua ne mihi scandala ponant
   Iniciantque thoro furta prophana meo.
Sic poterant calicem mihi supposuisse latenter
   Et mea terribili colla dedisse cruci.
925 Dissimulat pastor quicquid delinquit in me,
   Nemo ualet penis hunc satiare meis.
Vellet Sarmaticas essem procul actus in oras
   Quodque foret tellus ultima tyle mihi.
Dixerat in Syriam nuper me mittere uelle—
930 Nescio cur sacrum per mare tardat iter,
Si pax Assyrijs magnis si pax manet Indis,
   Indus et Assyrius quod mihi frater erit.

**Zelator:**
Mira referis, sed scire uelim quid transmare dignum
   Gesturus fueras, quod ne salutis opus.
935 Non licuit pungere tibi, nec barbara nosti
   Verba canum, celo nec bene suetus eras.

f. 178r [olim 177r]

---

910–18] om Me | 913 iudice] uindice Ot | 914 Qui] Quod Ot | 919 lacrimis adij] adji lacrimis Ot | 921 ponant] tendunt Me, uiros . . . ne] uiro . . . me Ot | 922–24] om Me | 923 latenter] latetri Ot | 925 delinquit] delinque Me, delinquitur Ot 927–29] om Me | 931 magnis] nigris Ot | 935 **pungere**] pungnare Ot, Me | 935 nec] ve Me

heaven. The shepherd is hardly in a position to care for his own flock if there was vengeance in your departure, which I do not believe. Perhaps the man was pleased to drive souls from his own territory (940) and to reveal his hurt feelings toward you. He believed he could assuage an injured spirit on the open sea and create new attitudes under a new sky.

But he believed wrongly. For past pain stains the heart with rust, no climates resolve anything. Anyone who crosses the sea changes his setting but not his soul. No land may have its own pilgrim. To condemn good men to exile is hardly ever an advantage. An exile considers the arrows of his resistance justified. Prison and exile are places for abundant meaning. (950) In prison or exile the injured breast fills up its quiver with arrows of revenge. Ovid was sent to the distant land of Tomis and there he felt fierce resentment. Caesar could tolerate neither the quivers nor the arrows, of which Ovid sent many from the Thracian shore. Whatever nasty things he saw in some secret hidden places he brought back to your senate, O Roman republic. Caesar could confine him to the icy Black Sea but could not get rid of him with aggressive weapons. Oh Caesar, you semi-divine soul, how much wiser you would be (960) if you had kept your man in the city. He would have fought for you, would have taken up arms on behalf of the citizens, he would have been ready to go anywhere in your empire. Then he might not have written what he brought to culpable light—which said nothing about the guilt of his exile.

Perhaps the abbot who is persecuting and harassing you is unworthy, distinguished by no pedigree. He is hard as iron and unfeeling of heart, as

---

945 Horace, *Epistles*, 1, 11, 27, where most modern editors put the verbs in the plural. | 951–64 Naso = Ovid (Publius Ovidius Naso), Tometane ... terre = of the territory around Tomis on the Black Sea, a reference to the *Tristia* and the *Ex ponto*. The poet develops the analogy of Ovid's exile and the abbot's threat of exile for the Persecutor.

*Liber de duobus monachis*

Si uindicta fuit quod non puto seuius ire
    Vix poterat pastor consuluisse sue.
Forte uiro placuit animos euincere terris
940    Et reuelare loco pectora lesa tibi.
Credidit offensam pelago componere mentem <sup>f. 178v</sup>
    Et noua sub celo corda creare nouo.
Credidit in uanum. Nam quod rubigine tinxit
    Cor dolor emeritus, climata nulla nouant.
945  Celum non animum mutat qui transmare currit.
    Terra peregrinum non habeat ulla suum,
Exilio dampnare bonos haut profuit unquam,
    Justa repugnandis spicula pulsus habet.
Carcer et exilium loca sunt pro diuite sensu.
950    Hic implent pharetras pectora lesa suas.
Naso Thometane fuit actus ad ultima terre,
    Nec tamen hic animis defuit ille feris.
Non potuit Cesar pharetras et spicula ferre
    Que sibi de Getico littore plura dedit.
955  Quicquid in occultis male uiderat ante latebris
    Iniecit theatris publica Roma tuis.
Quem potuit Cesar gelido constringere Ponto
    Non poterat telis euacuare feris.
O par semideum, quanto consultior esses,
960    Si tibi seruasses, Cesar, in urbe virum,
Pro te pugnasset, pro ciuibus arma tulisset, <sup>f. 179r [olim 178r]</sup>
    Isset ad imperium promptus et omne tuum.
Tunc neque scripsisset quid noxia lumina fecit,
    Que fuit exilij culpa tacenda sui.
965  Degener est forsan, et nullo stemmate clarus,
    Qui te persequitur exagitatque pater.
Ferreus est abbas et eodem pectore durus

---

937–44] om Me | 938] consuluisse] consiluisse Gh | 947 haut profuit] non obfuit Me | 948] om Me | 951–64] om Me | 956 theatris] rostris Co | 958 telis] elis Gh 962 omne] ubique Co | 963 lumina] limina Co | 964 tacenda] tacendi Co | 965 stemmate] stemate Co | 967] Me inserts after 950

the man who was immersed in the river Lethe. So he does not fear weapons or poisoned spears, (970) the dangers an Indian or a Saracen will give you. Let's imagine that he comes forth from Dis or the Acheron, and he may wish to fear nothing human. But he will dread you, for whom all heaven fights—you whom God saves everywhere with his power.

Oh greatly beloved of God whom God's own right hand saves from men filled with rancorous guile, believe me, in you the original miracles shine forth again and the olden days are returning with new signs. Behold! Once again God vindicates an innocent Susanna; (980) through you are dishonest priests exposed. Lo! Once again God has woven a cloak of many colours for you who extirpate the trickery of those brothers. These miracles would break the hardest of breasts; iron hearts may quake with fear at such omens. Witnesses to wickedness may assuage the penalties and the pain, but no judge can go unpunished for long. I hear that a harmful consumption is drying out the abbot's chest; a moist herbal remedy may give deserved ease to a pious old man whose moistness has dried out—(990) a dry illness is consuming a dry man.

But you meanwhile bear with all patience a sick master who has little time left. Go about your business cheerfully; if you are ordered to sea, go;

---

**968–69** If this is a reference to Achilles, then I suspect the poet changed the Styx to the Lethe on metrical grounds, for Stigio would give him two short syllables where he needed two long ones, which the adjective Letheo does give him. See Statius, *Achilleid*, ed. A. Marastoni, Bibliotheca Scriptorum Graecorum et Romanorum Teubneriana (Leipzig, 1974), l. 269-70, for a very brief account of how Thetis held Achilles by the heel and dipped him in the Styx to make him invulnerable. | **970** See note to 929. | **971** Dite > Dis, Pluto, cf. Vergil *Aeneid*, 6, 127, 269, 397, 541.

Quo qui Letheo tinctus in amne fuit,
Unde nec arma timet nec toxica tela ueretur,
970   Indus et Assyrius que tibi multa dabunt.
Esto quod ex Dite modo prodeat aut Acharonte
Humanumque nichil pertimuisse uelit.
Te tamen horrebit pro quo celestia pugnant,
Quem uirtute sua seruat ubique Deus.
975   O multum dilecte Deo, quem dextra Tonantis
Uindicat in plenis felle doloque uiris,
In te, crede michi, miracula prisca relucent
Et redeunt ueteres in noua signa dies.
Uindicat innocuam rursum Deus, ecce, Susannam,
980   Pro te presbyteros corripiendo malos.
Conpensat tunicam rursum Deus, en, polimitam,   f. 179v
Pro te fraternos excrutiando dolos.
Hec adamantinum frangant miracula pectus,
Talibus auspicijs ferrea corda tremant.
985   Nequitie testes penas soluere dolori,
Nec ualet impunis arbiter esse diu.
Audio quod thysis sua noxia pectora siccat,
Humida nec ualeat malua fouere senem
Et merito pietatis eum quem deserit humor,
990   Consumit siccum passio sicca uirum.
Tu tamen interea mentem dulcedine tota
Fer patienter herum, qui breue tempus habet.

---

Acharonte = Acheron, an underworld river, cf. Vergil *Aeneid*, 6, 7, 91, 107, 295, 312, 569—none of which seems to be a direct source. | **977–78** Reminiscent of Vergil *Eclogae*, 4, 6–7. | **979–80** Dan 13, 1–63, | **981** Gen 37, 3–4.

---

**968–69**] om **Me** | **968** Quo . . . tinctus] Quod . . . tractus **Co** | **969** timet . . . tela] om **Me**, 969 follows 970 **Me** | **970** multa] mille **Co**, mala **Me** | **973** Te tamen] Abbas **Me** | **974**] om **Me**, Quem] Que **Co** | **977–78**] om **Me** | **980**] om Me, Pro] Per **Co** **982**] om **Me**, Pro . . . excruciando] exutiendo **Gh**, Per . . . excrutiendo **Co** | **983** frangant] frangunt **Co** | **984–90**] om **Me** | **984** ferrea . . . tremant] ferra **Ot**, tremunt **Co** | **985** dolori] dolorum **Co** | **987** sua] sibi **Co** | **988** nec ualeat] sic ualet **Co**

don't let any climate give you difficulties. Conceal patiently whatever wrong he does against you; a just God will reward patience.

But I would really like to know the original root or starting point of this plague. I would ask you then to explain these things further to me, but expound them in a few words—(1000) that speaker is best who can be brief.

**Persecutor:**
My suffering is both brief and long, my good friend, brief to relate but long in the suffering. There was one among us who, having turned his back on being a monk, donned episcopal vestments. A man of no land, no title, no throne, no particular place, but merely a servant—he was called Symon. For a long time he tried to flatter me, and he gave secret advice to my abbot, namely that I should become the abbot's colleague. And so it was done—(1010) and altogether my mind, my heart, and my hand approved. Immediately we set sail in a tempestuous wind and entered unknown waters, like the bay of the Gethi and the Sarmatici. Here I recalled Ovid when I saw the monsters, whose faces were created with long hair. We roamed and wandered, unstable over lands and seas, seeking favourable fortune everywhere. Fortune did not favour us, but rather we were rejected everywhere, we took the utmost insults and ridicule of the crowd.

Poverty, you horrible plague! (1020) A noble bishop stands decorated with precious metal—I stand barefoot. Symon sat on a discarded sack, and reproaching us rather sharply, spoke seriously: 'Why are you useless

---

996 Walther, *Prov*, p. 740. | 1012 Ovid *Ex ponto*, 1, 5, 62. | 1014 Reminiscent of Ovid *Tristia*, 5, 7, 11–18.

---

994–95] om **Me** | 996 iustus . . . Deus] Deus . . . iustus **Me** | 997–1000] om **Me** 998 quel uel] vel que **Co** | 999 Hec . . . dicere] Hec rogo . . . digere **Co**, Hoc **Ot**

Omnia letus agas, mare si iubearis, adito,
    Dent tibi difficiles climata nulla uias.
995 Dissimula patiens quidquid delinquitur in te,
    Redditor est iustus pro patiente Deus.
Scire tamen uellem radix que prima fuisset
    Istius morbi que uel origo mali.
Hec mihi depromas et paucis dissere uerbis—
1000     Optimus est rethor qui breuis esse potest.

**Persecutor:**

f. 180r [olim 179r]

Est breuis et longa mea passio, blande sodalis—
    Ore quidem breuis est longa dolore tamen.
Qui spreto monacho sibi pontificalia sumunt—
    Ex hijs in nobis patribus vnus erat.
1005 Nulla uiro tellus, titulusque, thronusque, locusque—
    Sed tantum seruus, nomine Symon erat.
Iste michi longo blandiri tempore cepit,
    Abbatique meo munera ceca dedit,
Scilicet socius fierem patris. Hoc ita facto,
1010     Accessere tribus mens, cor, et vna manus.
Haut mora thyphonico laxamus carbasa uento,
    Intramus Gethicos Sarmaticosque sinus.
Hic ego Nasonis memini, cum monstra uiderem,
    Ora quibus longis creta fuere comis.
1015 Currimus instabiles terris erramus et vndis,
    Querimus in cunctis prospera fata locis.
Nil nobis fortuna fauet, sed ubique repulsi
    Opprobrium uulgi ridiculumque summus.
Paupertas, horrenda lues! Stat sub ere cinctus
1020     Nobilis antistes, sto pede nudus ego.
Symon in abiecto sacco sedet, acrius ergo    f. 180v

---

1001 Est] Et **Me** | 1002 Ore . . . tamen] Que . . . nimis **Me** | 1004 patribus] pater **Me** | 1005 thronusque titulusque] tytulusque thorusque **Me** | 1007 Iste] Ipse **Me** 1008–14] om **Me**, added line: Vt exeam promittit incomoda multa instabilas **Me** 1010 accessere] accressere **Ot** | 1017 nobis] uotis **Gh Co**, notis **Ot** | 1018 summus] damur **Co, Me** | 1019] om **Me** | 1020 Nobilis] nudis **Me**

people so feckless and lazy about everything? Is it right that priests of Christ should perish like this? The mother of logic and the sophists were often destitute; in such tight circumstances nothing much helps—and that's why we are here. But God be with you, I have never as I grew older seen drooping faces on rich people. I am not so slow, though tending toward old age, (1030) let me not be an honest servant to some bishop. I shall set forth; I shall be a fisherman; I shall test the deeps; I know pools that have yet to feel a net. Even though the nets are not yet ready to hand, the great hooked staff of authority is best—the ring and the mitre, the religious appearance of a priest, the simplicity of a brother will catch the sea monsters.'

Action followed the words; we blessed the site, destroyed the old altars, and built new ones. We anointed priests and ovens with one and the same chrism, (1040) and there was no end to our holy artifice. Corruption, buying and selling, fraud, cheating on agreements—these were the nets with which our kitchen was heated. From this point on our culture was blessed, from this point on we had splendid silks and satins, from this point on fat bellies, from this point on our hands were heavy with gold.

All our success happened through Symon's cleverness; our cloister grew with generous gifts. We had washerwomen, vines, and there were girls whom a short needle adapted to the elegance of our leader. Which of us was now poorer than Codrus the pauper? (1050) Every sort of servant of the community was put under our authority. Here a brother collecting holy incense and candle wax—his little acts of theft light up his

---

1025 logices, Greek genitive. | 1048 breuis … acus = embroidery? Or an obscenity? For obscene meanings of acus, see Carissa M. Harris, "'Yt was a woman or a womans thing': Neglected Obscene Riddles in CUL MS. Dd.5.75," *Journal of the Early Book Society*, 22 (2019), 213–23. | 1049 paupere Codro, cf. Juvenal 3, 208–11.

1022] om Me, monet] mouet Co | 1023 torpetis] torpemus Me | 1024–29] om Me

*Liber de duobus monachis*

Improperans nobis hec monet ore graui:
'Quid uos degeneres torpetis ad omnia pigri?
Prespiteros Christi sicne perire decet?
1025 Sepe mater logyces inopesque fuere sophiste,
Rebus in angustis nil ualet, ergo sumus.
Ast nunquam, dominus uobiscum, marcida uidi
Ut senui diuis ora dedisse uiris.
Non adeo sum lentus, adhuc vergente senecta,
1030 Pontificis seruus ne probus esse queam.
Egrediar, piscator ero, temptabo profundum,
Stagna scio nullis anticipata plagis.
Etsi non presto sunt instrumenta laboris,
Pontificis baculus optimus hamus erit—
1035 Anulus et mitra, frons patris religiosa,
Simplicitas socij monstra marina trahent.'
Res sequitur uerbum: loca sanctificamus et aras
Destruimus ueteres erigimusque nouas.
Uno presbiteros et eodem crismate furnos
1040 Ungimus, et non est finis in arte sacra.
Corruptela, forum, fraus, circumuencio pactum—
Retia sunt per que nostra coquina calet.
Hinc sacer est cultus, hinc nobis splendida byssus,
Hinc uenter pinguis, hinc manus ere grauis.
1045 Symonis ingenio succedunt prospera cuncta.
Augetur uarijs curia nostra bonis.
Lotrices vinee sunt nobis, suntque puelle
Presulis ad cultum quas breuis aptat acus.
Qui modo plus tenues fueramus paupere Codro?
1050 Seruorum nobis subditur omne genus.

f. 181r [olim 180r]

---

1025 mater] macri **Ot** | 1026 sumus] suum **Ot**, sum **Co** | 1027 Ast] At **Co** | 1029 Non adeo] Nam adero **Co** | 1030 probus] probet **Co** | 1032–33] om **Me** | 1033 laboris] sagene **Co** | 1034 optimus hamus] hamus optimus **Ot**, **Me** | 1035–36] om **Me** | 1035 patris] patri **Co** | 1037 uerbum] verbo **Me** | 1039 furnos] firmos **Me** 1041 fraus] firmus **Me** | 1042 Retia] retiaque **Co** | 1043 sacer] satis **Co** | 1044 ere] ecce **Co** | 1045–46] om **Me** | 1048 cultum] cultura **Gh** | 1049 plus] autem **Me**

eyes. A second brother, accustomed to more serious fraud, asks for a financial contribution in his chalice, or else he demands a more substantial sum In the form of a pledge. Yet a third brother strips altars of their legitimate hangings—let him hang onto his book as his right by gift. Still another demands his rights with the authority of his seal, without which no document has any authority. And there is yet another brother who, while carrying the sacred reliquary, (1060) tears away a piece of agate or even such a jewel as a red stork might lay.

What do you suppose is the source of the onyxes and the green emeralds, many of which grace Symon's thieving hands? Why do I hesitate? Even if there are contacts with thousands of clients, it would still not be right to reveal anyone's identity. In my mind I did not want to know what they were scarcely able to say, those who had been put to flight and beaten with rods. Symon's blameworthy fishing expeditions came thick and fast, and I said to the brothers, 'Get away from these fishing holes! In such a river such fish are caught. (1070) As a wave washes the hands, so sin washes the theft of consecrated gifts.' I did what I recommended. I left both Symon and the father, returned to my cloister, and resumed the life that I had had before. However, that treacherous Symon was able to inflict his tricks on me even after I left—you cannot guess how, but from that hook hangs the burden of all my woe; from that root springs all my suffering.

**Zelator:**
Hide nothing, dearly beloved, but finish what you started, and tell us of Symon's treachery and malice. I have heard about his deceit, that he often

---

1060 conea = ciconia. The agate in the preceding line may have brought to the poet's mind the myth of the stork laying an agate. Cf. Petrus Alfonsi, *Disciplina clericalis*, ed. A. Hilka and W. Söderhjelm (Heidelberg, 1911), p. 33, ll. 37–38 and the account of the agate in 'Physiologus latinus versio Y', Francis Carmody, ed., *Classical Weekly*, 35 (1941), 95–134, at p. 120

---

1051–52] om Me | 1055–56] om Me | 1057 Alter] Ater Co, sua] sui Me | 1058–64]

Hic aliquis sacra thura legens et cerea carpens—
    Lumina dant oculis furta pusilla suis.
Alter maiori consuetus fraude talentum
    Postulat in calicem, uel graue pignus agit.
1055 Hic est qui pallis altaria nudet ademptis—
    Librum detineat pro ratione dati.
Alter ab impresso poscit sua iura sigillo,
    Uis instrumenti quo sine nulla ualet.
Est alius qui, dum sacra scrinia portat, achatem
1060     Eripit autem gemmam quam rubra conea parit.
Unde, putas, ueniant onyces uiridesque smaragdi,   f. 181v
    Quas gestat multas Symonis vnca manus?
Quid moror? Et si sint contagia mille clientum,
    Non tamen ad lucem singula ferre decet.
1065 Hoc te unum scire nolo quod sepe fugati
    Et baculis cesi uix potuere loqui.
Symonis hec culpata michi piscatio crebro est,
    Et dixi pueris, 'Hos fugitote lacus!
In tali tales capiuntur flumine pisces.
1070     Noxia sacrilegas sic lauat vnda manus.'
Quod docui feci. Symonemque patremque reliqui,
    Redditus et claustro, sum ueluid ante meo.
Attamen insidias michi quas post terga tetendit
    Perfidus iste Symon, non modo scire potes,
1075 Pendet in hoc clauo totius sarcina morbi,
    Hac radice meus pullulat ille dolor.

**Zelator:**
Ne taceas, dilecte comes, sed perfice ceptum,
    Et dic insidias Symonis atque dolos.
Audiui de fraude uiri quod sepe potentes

---

om Me | 1060 conea] concha Ot | 1061 ueniant] ueniunt Co | 1063 moror] maior Ot, si sint] sistat Co | 1065 te unum] in mente Co | 1067–68] om Me | 1070] 1068 inserted here Me | 1072 Redditus et . . . meo] redditur . . . modo Co | 1073–74] om Me | 1074 scire] sine Co | 1077 Ne taceas] nec celes Ot, Co, Non celes Me | 1079 uiri] sua Co

(1080) pushed aside powerful abbots and consecrated bishops, but since you are a humble person and not one of his party, I wonder what Symon could have done to affect your destiny. Perhaps you took bits and pieces of Symon with you back to your cloister, and you are not yet free of his influence? For his peculiarities run alongside Symon, and both monsters, you and he, go at an equal pace. Symon has overthrown both bishops and tall mitres, and his influence harms simple monks. This is the wretched plague, this is the curse of Gehazi, (1090) this produces leprosy but has an image as white as snow. Oh Maccabees, this is the calamity, this the monetary disgrace hiding under your tunics!

Recently a terrible thing, a shocking incident happened, alas and woe is me, in my own cloister. A certain lay brother had reached the point where he needed to receive the last rites. The brothers gathered around, with Peter carrying the osculatory—the cross preceded, bearing its exalted treasures on high. Peter sprinkled holy water about the house and drove the ghosts away, (1100) he drove the airy pestilences from the land with incense. Consecrated candles drove off the terrors of darkness; whatever can do harm departed through the power of prayer. And after anointing the sensitive region of the head, the abbot came to the man's loins. Here between the buttocks a money bag heavy with metal was hanging just as, I think, a bag sometimes holds a sum of money. Seeing this the holy

---

**1089–90** IV Reg 5:20-27. Yezi (Giezi, Gehazi) is often identified as a type of simony, selling sacraments that should be freely given. Cf. St Augustine *Ad fratres in eremo sermo 37*, PL 40: 1301–04. Cf. Walter of Châtillon *The Shorter Poems*, ed. and trans. D.A. Traill, Oxford Medieval Texts (Oxford, 2013), poem 14, 4, 2; 44, 31, 3; 48, 13, 1; 64, 29, 6, and Traill's comments on p. liv. | **1092** gens Machabea = Symon. Cf. I Mach 2:3. Cf. also II Mach 5:21 and 9:2, for the association with stolen wealth. **1097** tabellam = an osculatory, a flat piece of wood either painted or carved with an image of Jesus, formerly kissed by the priest during mass. All three MSS agree in reading 'feriente', which scans, though the more correct 'ferente' does not. But cf. the Medieval Latin feriare, which could have caused some confusion. | **1098–1128** For similar stories see Caesarius of Heisterbach *Dialogus miraculorum*, ed. J. Strange (Cologne, 1851), II, pp. 302-4, dist. 11, cap. 43–45; A.G. Little, *Liber exemplorum*

| 1080 | Submouet abbates pontificesque sacros, |
| | At tu cum modicus nec sis de partibus unus, <sup>f. 182r [olim 181r]</sup> |
| | Miror quid potuit in tua fata Symon. |
| | Forsitan ad claustrum tecum fragmenta tulisti |
| | Symonis, et nondum proprietate cares. |
| 1085 | Denique proprietas vna cum Symone currit, |
| | Et faciunt passus utraque monstra pares. |
| | Symon pontifices et cornua deicit alta, |
| | Proprietas monachis simplicibusque nocet. |
| | Hec est plaga nocens, hec est maledictio Yezi, |
| 1090 | Inducens lepram ut niuis instar habet. |
| | Hec est pernicies, hec est eraria labes, |
| | Illatitans tunicis gens Machabea tuis. |
| | Quiddam terribile nuper plenumque stupore |
| | Accidit in claustro, proch dolor ecce, meo. |
| 1095 | Uenerat articulum quidam conuersus ad illum |
| | Quod sibi debebat vnctio sacra dari. |
| | Conueniunt fratres, Petro feriente tabellam, |
| | Crux preit in capite digna throphea gerens. |
| | Aspergit sacra linfa domum Lemuresque repellit, |
| 1100 | Aereas pestes thuris a terra fugat. |
| | Lumina terrores tenebrarum sacra repellunt, <sup>f. 182v</sup> |
| | Vi precis abscedit quicquid obesse potest. |
| | Etiam sensifica capitis regione peruncta, |
| | Abbas ad lumbos uenerat usque uiri. |
| 1105 | Hic inter clunes grauis ere crumena pependit |

---

*ad usum praedicantium* (Aberdeen, 1908), pp. 10–11; T.F. Crane, ed., *The Exempla of Jacques de Vitry* (repr. Liechtenstein, 1967), pp. 74–75.

1080 Submouet] Submoveat **Me** | 1081–82] Om **Me** | 1081 nec sis de partibus unus] cunctis nouissimus extes **Co** | 1084 nondum] non **Me** | 1086] om **Me** | 1086 utraque] ultraque **Ot** | 1089–92] om **Me** | 1099 Aspergit] Asparget **Me** | 1100–02] om **Me** | 1101 lumina] om **Gh**, terrores tenebrarum sacra repelunt] demonium sacra pellunt meridianum **Co** | 1102 Vi . . . obesse] Ut . . . abesse **Co** | 1105 ere . . . pependit] ecce **Co**, pendebat, om ere **Me**

father said, 'Brethren, come closer and see what this swelling in the loins means.' For the innocent man believed that perhaps beneath his shaggy groin (1110) there might have been a hernia or a painful haemorrhoid. The brothers moved quickly and unfastened the puckering strings of the purse. And they shake out money! Coins rush forth, the ground bristles with them. The earth shudders and is stunned at the coins, stamped with many faces of heroes, the appearance of foreign dukes. Here are those whom a profile of the first Belus decorated, here those which the stern face of Numa inscribed. While they are destroying the coins and their images, the spirit left the mouth of the avaricious man. Immediately the abbot orders that the sinful man's corpse (1120) be dragged into a vast cave filled with wild animals. 'Go,' he says, 'and fill the breast of the miser with coins. His money may help the filthy capitalist. Let him who lived privately for himself be deprived of a funeral, a tomb, a candle, incense, prayer.' This sinful capitalist still disturbs us at night and frightens us with his long testicle-purse and his harsh voice, for he often shouts to us: 'Take me up out of this filthy pit, put me in a proper coffin, and I will give you five talents.'

So an evil nature may still stick to Symon, (1130) and usually there is a single sorry outcome for both Symon and his evil nature. Tell us then all the malice and expose Symon's fraudulent doings. Let no man hesitate to expose the nefarious deeds of humans. There are still prudential moves for good men and fearful things for evil ones, and thus an evil cause may yet

---

1115 Cf. Vergil, *Aeneid* 1, 729. This is probably not Dido's father (*Aen.* 1, 621), but a more ancient Belus, perhaps a Carthaginian. Here, like Numa in the following line, an example of the sort of dux (975) whose image might be stamped on a coin. | 1116 Perhaps Numa Pompilius, mentioned in Ovid *Fasti*, 2, 69, the second king of Rome, also one whose image might appear on a coin.

*Liber de duobus monachis*

        Ut, reor, in summa quandoque talenta tenens.
    Quam pater, ut uidit, 'Fratres, accedite,' dixit,
        'Querite lumborum quid tumor iste uelit.'
    Crediderat simplex quod forte sub inguine toruo
1110      Ernya nata foret yliacusque dolor.
    Accelerant prompti, burseque repagula soluunt,
        Excutiunt nummos: es ruit, horret humus!
    Horret humus nummosque stupet quos multa sigillat
        Heroum facies, extera forma ducum.
1115   Hic sunt quos prisci signarat formula Beli,
        Hic quos inscripsit torua figura Nume.
    Spiritus interea, dum res lacerantur et era,
        Egressus cupidi liquerat ora uiri.
    Haut mora defunctum mandat preceptor iniquum
1120      Bestibus iniectis uasta sub antra trahi.
    'Ite,' ait, 'et nummis infundite pectus auari.    f. 183r [olim 182r]
        Nummicolam nummus adiuuet ille suus.
    Qui sibi priuatim uixit priuetur et ipse
        Exequijs, tumba, lumine, thure, prece.'
1125   Vexat adhuc noctu nos proprietarius iste
        Et terret longo teste sonoque truci.
    Clamat enim crebro, 'Putei me tollite ceno,
        Ponite sarcophago, quinque talenta dabo.'
    Sic mala proprietas cum Symone currit, et unus
1130      Amborum tristis exitus esse solet.
    Pande dolos, igitur, et Symonis edito fraudes,
        Impia facta hominum nemo tacenda putet.
    Sunt equidem cautela bonis formido malignis;

---

1109–10] om **Me** | 1110 Ernya] Heria **Co** | 1112 nummos . . . humus] loculos **Ot**, horror **Co**, humo **Me** | 1113 Horret humus nummosque stupet quos] Sacrilegum nummisma cadit quod **Co** | 1113–16] om **Me** | 1115 prisci signarat] primi signauit **Co** | 1117 interea . . . era] interitus **Co**, bursa **Me** | 1120 Bestibus] Restibus **Ot**, **Me** 1121 auari] auarum **Co** | 1121–22] om **Me** | 1122 adiuuet] adiuuat **Co** | 1123 priuatim] priuate **Me** | 1126] inserted after 1128 **Me** | 1128 talenta] talentam **Me**, **Me** adds extra line: Eiectum corpus in mare mersimus illud | 1131] om **Me**, edito] edite **Co** | 1132 tacenda] cauenda **Co** | 1133 formido malignis] cavenda malignus **Me**

produce good results. There are three things that no man ever successfully hides: illness, poverty, and a seriously wounded heart. Explain your illness to your doctor; I attribute your poverty to circumstance; and tell your friend your heart, revealing everything.

**Persecutor:**
Let me continue with my story, for you are surrounding me with explanations (1140) and yet you sympathise with my problems. When I returned to my cloister, Symon's trickery followed after me—not in person, but he did set his sacrilegious hands to work. First he circulated a well-known libel against me, a libel whose title reflected the character of its author. But lest you are in any doubt about that document, this was the gist of it from start to finish:

'To the abbot of Vacarinensis, may he enjoy his well-deserved prosperity, his own Symon sends greetings. Since our Christian faith, together with many favours received, binds us together, (1150) as does our indissoluble affection, I do not wish—nay, I cannot, I must not remain silent about the losses which are about to harm you, my lord. That chaplain of ours—the very one who deserted us, do you know why he fled? Why he deserted us? Why he left our brotherhood? Now, gentle father, may it help you to learn, to know the character, the customs, and the names of the brothers: it is characteristic of the shepherd to get the praise, of the flock to get the benefit.

'Recently this fellow dreamt that he was elevated to the stars and (1160) almost to a pontifical mitre made for himself. Swollen with this excrescence, though without the crown itself, he impetuously set forth: but actually a priest's modest dress is more suitable for him. It is not

---

1143 This famous libellus evidently exists only in the version quoted here, ll. 1147–1208. | 1147 For possible identities of Vacaranensi, see Introduction, p. xxiii. 1153 capellanus = Persecutor.

Et sic effectus dat mala causa bonos.
1135 Sunt tria que celat nullus feliciter unquam:
   Morbus, pauperies, cor graue uulnus habens.
Dic morbum medico, defectum rebus opinio,
   Cor graue dic socio te reuelanda suo.
**Persecutor:**
Prosequar inceptum, quia me rationibus artas,
1140   At tu iacture compatiare mee.
Symon, ut ad claustrum redij, me fraude secutus      f. 183v
   Non pede, sacrilegas misit ad arma manus.
Denique famosum dedit in mea fata libellum,
   Cuius erat titulus qualis et auctor erat.
1145 Sed ne iam dubium te reddat epistula missa,
   De uerbo ad uerbum sic tenor eius erat:
'Abbati Vacaranensi suus ille salutem
   Symon et optata prosperitate frui.
Cum sincera fides cum gratia multa fauoris
1150   Nos liget et societ inuiolatus amor,
Nec uolo nec possum nec debeo dampna silere,
   Que uobis domino sunt nocitura meo.
Ille capellanus noster, desertor et idem—
   An nescitis adhuc que sibi causa fuge?
1155 Cur nos deseruit? Cur federa nostra reliquit?
   Nunc, mansuete pater, uos didicisse iuuat,
Noscere personas, mores, et nomina fratrum:
   Laus est pastoris utilitasque gregis.
Uiderat in sompnis se nuper ad ardua raptum
1160   Et quasi pontificis cornua nata sibi.      f. 184r [olim 183r]
Hac tumidus struma dum rem minus impetuose

---

1134] om Me, dat] dant Ot, Co | 1135 celat . . . unquam] nunquam Ot, tolerat Co, nullus celat Me | 1138 te releuanda tuo] presbiteroque bono Co, Me | 1144–46] om Me | 1147 Vacaranensi . . . ille] uacare mensas Symon Co, vacaremensi Symon ego Me | 1148 Symon] Simul Me | 1149 sincere] sui causa Me | 1151-55] om Me | 1153 noster] uester Co | 1159–1202] Uiderat . . . manus] En frater ille fur est et loculos habet Me | 1161 dum rem] de re Co

really modest, however, for he has soiled himself with theft and you and the brothers and his cloister at the same time. He is a frivolous and vain man: while he snatches at dreams of honour, he broke into the treasury with the magic art of enchantment. He removed the splendid tiara with its jewels and gold, one so fine that the pope himself scarcely bears a finer one on his head. (For this was the very mitre which our right hand conferred upon the father (1170) when he was made Primate.) As a thief is usually terrified in his mind and well aware of his guilt, even as he trembles to hide his theft in various places, what does he do? He puts the loot in a pig pen, he defiles sacred treasure. He commends the sacred mitre of the father to a pig pen! The treasure that was sought everywhere—for shame—was finally found, recognised by its thousand muddy stains. It came to light not by chance but as it were by God's will and judgement. A sow, having given birth, protected her piglets, (1180) as is the custom with swine, by building a nest in just such a place. I don't know what sort of scrap there may have been between some dogs and the sow, perhaps she turned furious in defence of her young. But when she rounded on the dogs with her savage sharp teeth, she dug into the ditch with her hooves and the blessed treasure with its jewels was revealed.

'The lads ran up, seized the abbot's mitre, and brought it to my gaze. It was filthy, and it assailed our noses with a vile odour, now totally unsuitable for holy use. As soon as the father saw this he said, "What a sacrilegious crime! (1190) In Christ our Lord, who dared to do this? What has light got to do with darkness? Or what agreement between Christ and Satan? Or what alliance of dogs with sacred articles? The

---

1163 mala ... et] male ... in **Ot**, parca **Co** | 1168 sancto] summos **Co** | 1173 Intrat ... cedit] Obscene rem ponit in ore cloace **Co** | 1174 Commendat ... patris] Inter podiscos sordidulosque globos **Co** | 1175 nausea tandem] dedecus **Co** | 1176 Est ... notis] Latrine tandem scena reperta fuit **Co** | 1177 a casu ... diuino] ex casu diuino

Adgreditur: patris est infula parta sibi.
Est mala parta tamen, nam furto polluit et se
  Et uos et fratres et sua claustra simul.
1165 Vir leuis et vanus, dum sompnia captat honoris,
  Dissoluit magici carminis arte seram.
Subtrahit insignem gemmis auroque tyaram,
  Qualem uix sancto uertice papa gerit.
(Ipsa fuit mitra quam patri dextera nostra
1170  Imposuit primam quando creatus erat.)
Fur mentis pauide male conscius ut solet esse,
  Dum timet in cunctis condere furta locis.
Quid facit? Intrat aram porcis sacra pignera cedit
  Commendat stabulo cornua sacra patris.
1175 Res cunctis quesita locis, proch nausea, tandem
  Est inventa luti mille notata notis.
Non tamen a casu sed diuino quasi nutu
  Iudicioque Dei, res manifesta datur.
Sus fetus enixa suos consueuerat illo,
1180  Ut mos est porcis, nidificare loco.
Nescio que canibus tunc cum sue bella fuere— f. 184v
  Forsitan ob fetus seuijt illa suos.
Cumque truci rotat ore canes rigidoque, profundat
  Ungue scrobem, gemmis res patet alma suis.
1185 Accurrunt pueri, rapiuntque feruntque mitellam
  Patris, ad aspectus intuitusque meos.
Sorduit et diro nares infecit odore—
  Amodo iam sacris usibus apta nichil.
Quam pater ut uidit, "Tantum scelus impia!" dixit,
1190  "In Christum Dominum que manus ausa fuit?
Qui luci ad tenebras? Uel que conuencio Christi
  Ad Belial? Sanctis federa queue canum?

---

sed **Co** | 1180 mos] mors **Co** | 1186 intuitusque] nitueritque **Co** | 1187 Sorduit . . . odore] Heserunt hinc inde globi teretesque trocisi **Co** | 1188 Amodo . . . nichil] Pro nate dat quales stupea massa loco **Co** | 1189 pater . . . dixit] simul ut vidi . . . dixit **Co** | 1190 Dominum] domini **Ot**, **Co** | 1191 qui] quid **Co**

perpetrator of this defilement was no meritorious catholic, not even a pagan idolater, but Satan's own self! May a suitable pain strike this man who has stained not only sacred articles and the abbot but actually God himself." Holy Father, you may have feared just this, if anything of the golden mitre remains for your successors, for nothing trivial is (1200) normally stolen but only that which looks worthy of holy abbots. He has more regal treasures than you have, if you remember any of it. By no means a fugitive, he is however grim and so sour in his manner that none of our servants knows how to keep him in check, for three outstanding men recently deserted us—no one in the world was equal to them in cleverness. After these things had happened in this way, I could not tell everything no matter how fast I wrote. But the messenger knows the details.'

After scrutinizing the accusations of this untruthful libel, (1210) he gave it to the brothers for their inspection. 'Seize the man,' they cried. A judge stood next to the shouting mob, whom money moved more than if there was at least a tribunal. There was only a search for the money bags that damaged me. I could be sent away, unless there was a delay in looking for those money bags. The abbot was searching for the money bags through which he might exercise control to some degree. If there was anything hidden, he would give it to the gods and the lords. And then the man often known for his serious faults ought to have left the place long

---

1193 modo ... profanus] bene catholicus meriti blasphemus iniquus Co | 1194 Set . . . erat] Huius spurcicie fautor et auctor erat Co | 1195 feriat que] fiant Co | 1199 perspexerit] prospexerit Co | 1202 Haut . . . fugitura] hanc fugitiua Co | 1203 toruus] tornis Ot | 1205 primi . . . deseruere] servi Me, deseruisse Ot | 1206–30 Par quibus . . . vincla subi] Tunc michi abbas cur quid audio de te Me | 1207 decursis . . . usu] digestio . . . usus Co | 1208 poteram] poterat Co | 1209–22 Abbas mendosi . . . triginta uiri]

 Abbas, pestiferi discussa labe libelli,
  Quam uigili corde corruit inde notam!
 Quo pede contriuit facinus, quo pollice rupit

*Liber de duobus monachis*

     Non modo catholicus nec adhuc ydolatra prophanus,
        Set Satanas sedes hic malefactor erat.
1195  Passio digna uirum feriat qui non sacra solum
        Nec modo pontificem polluit immo Deum."
     Istud idem, reuerende pater, timuisse potestis,
        Si qua manet uestris aurea mitra seris,
     Nam nichil exiguum sed quod perspexerit almis
1200     Presulibus dignum corripuisse solet.
     Plurima sunt illi regum donaria uestras,   f. 185r [olim 184r]
        Si quicquam sapitis. Haut fugitura manus
     Preterea est toruus ita moribus acer, ut ipsum
        Seruorum nullus sustinuisse queat,
1205  Tres etenim primi nos nuper deseruere,
        Par quibus ingenio nullus in orbe fuit.
     Hjis ita decursis, uelocis arundinis usu
        Singula non poteram, cetera lator habet.'
     Abbas mendosi perspecta piacula libri,
1210     Fratribus hijs etiam perspicienda dedit
     'Tolle uirum,' clamant. Iudex clamantibus astat
        Quem si iudicium plus tamen era mouent.
     Sola fuit que me loculorum questio lesit.
        Dimitti poteram, que nisi mora foret.
1215  Querebat loculos per quos regnaret a parte
        Si quid in occulto dijs dominisque daret.
     Denique pro grauibus culpis uir sepe notatus

---

     Codicis infami[j]s crimina falsa, putas.
Uere non aliter exclusit crimen et hostem
     Quam qui sponte lupo pandit ouile suum.
Non aliter fame nostroque pepercit honori
     Quam solet ancille parcere leno rudi,
Scilicet obscenas quam postquam traxit,
     Et docuit castis depuduisse modis.
Inuitat ciues et ei cui mille parauit
     Parcit, adhuc tenere dimidiatque uiros.
Sic michi dimidians conuentum pessimus abbas
     Imposuit centum pene triginta uiros. **Co**

ago. But the shrewd fellow, (1220) the fingers of scribes and the helping hands of bishops, stands firm for his reward. And so I am called to the chapter house, which is marked by trickery, where some 130 men await me.

Before the group this serpent, wielding his thousand poisons and concealing his venom in dust, burst forth—oh horrible!—with the following: 'Come now, reveal yourself. It is enough that you have lain hidden for so many years. Now you are here, wear this well-deserved mark of your disgrace on your forehead. Come forth into the midst of these men, let your face, up to now invisible, be seen, you rapacious thief. Put your two hands into your treasure chests, and either return what was buried (1230) or suffer the fierce chains of a very harsh prison. Of your own free will confess your crime. Confession has done many men good, even when they endured a brief penance. Thus the sinful Achan confessed to Joshua, and his punishment was executed forthwith. But lest perhaps you think that your dream was true, the dream of wearing the episcopal mitre and stole, you can take off right now the insignia of our habit, rise up out of this congregation and go away. Be the last in the choir, the lowest at table, (1240) and may short rations consume your cheeks. Be silent, you confounded clod, don't let your own voice be heard in any peaceful and decent council. This respite will not last long for you—only until we can finish our dinner. After that, if you fail to show us your money bags and the gold, you will be held, as I said, fettered in prison.'

And then it was time to dine; soft cushions held the abbot, a mind deeply trusting in God held me. Oh boundless goodness of God, what

---

**1226** Cf. Apoc 13:16. | **1233–34** Ios 7:18-25.

Olim debuerat deseruisse locum
Callidus ipse tamen stat per sua munera firmus
1220     Ungues scribarum pontificumque manus.
Ergo cauillosa uocor ad capitolia quo me     f. 185v
    Expectant centum pene triginta uiri.
Hijs coram prorupit in hoc, o dire, cerastes
    Mille venena gerens, puluere dypsa latens:
1225 'Nunc age, prode caput. Satis est latuisse tot annis.
    Huc ades, et meritas accipe fronte notas.
In medios procede uiros, da cernere uultus
    Hactenus inuisos, fur truculente, tuos.
Ad duo mitte manus loculos, uel redde sepultos
1230     Carceris extremi uel fera vincla subi.
Sponte tuum fateare scelus. Confessio multis
    Profuit et penam sustinuere breuem.
Sic Iosue sceleratus Achor detexit, et eius
    Mox in momento pena peracta fuit.
1235 Sed ne iam fortasse putes tua somnia uera,
    De mitra imposita pontificisque stola,
Exue festinus habitus insignia nostri,
    A cetu fratrum surge, recede procul.
Ultimus in stallo mensa postremus adesto,
1240     Consumat genas arta dieta tuas.
Confusus sileas, tua uox autentica non sit     f. 186r [olim 185r]
    Quolibet in placito consilioque bono.
Nec tamen ista tibi durabit gratia multum,
    Sed dum finiri prandia nostra queant.
1245 Postque, si loculos non demonstrabis et aurum,
    Carceris, ut dixi, compede tentus eris.'
Et iam tempus erat prandendi; mollia patrem

1222 expectant], . . . uiri] Inposuit . . . uiros **Co** | 1223 hoc] hec **Co** | 1224 dypsa] diploma **Co** | 1233 sic . . . eius] Se **Gh**, sceleratum **Co**, petam **Me** | 1234–37] om **Me** | 1235 Sed . . . putes] Se **Gh**, putas **Co** | 1239 mensa . . . adesto] mensaque nouissimus esto **Co**, **Me**, esto **Gh** | 1240 genas] buccas **Co**, **Me** [for 1242, **Me**, f. 62r: substitutes 1230] | 1242–58] om **Me**

great trust they have (1250) who hope in your benevolence! The contented abbot was dining in the summery hall, and as usual there was a sumptuous table spread for him. Who usually dines better or more sumptuously than those whose groins and bellies have been dutifully cared for? After serving everything else, finally a platter full of marrow bones was brought before the abbot. The cook had baked delicious marrow in a slow oven and had scattered ground and chopped spices over it. The abbot having cleared his throat was rising to reach for the bones, (1260) when a fragment of food entered his throat crossways; the lethal morsel went astray and stuck in his gullet, right where the windpipe lies open. His esophagus was blocked—then he erupted with an enormous gasp—he certainly couldn't remember the promised prison.

His burial was still going on, not yet covered with soft earth, when there arrived an unexpected messenger sent by sea. He reported that the bishop had been killed in the slaughter of the Lapiths and that Symon had been captured and jailed. It was Symon's boy who brought these orders (1270) to the abbot, on the assumption that he was still alive. He was looking for the hidden treasures and was asking the abbot who, for goodness sake, was Symon's treasurer and keeper of the strongbox. The whole affair was revealed in our midst. The group of brothers was amazed and fearful. 'Woe unto us,' they exclaimed, 'is the abbot now lost? Is he well past redemption?' For if he ran with the thief, he could be damned

---

1267 Cf. Ovid *Metamorphoses*, 12, 210–535. It is difficult to explain just how a reference to the wedding of Pirithous and Hippodame serves to make negative line 1268, but the context seems to establish Symon's escape from the clutches of authority, for he has sent his servant to reclaim all the goods he stole during his fund-raising drive (1037–64). Perhaps one explanation might be that the servant tells that the bishop has been killed in some sort of infighting (caedes Laphitarum), leaving Symon free to continue with his exploits. If that is so, then the Persecutor's

*Liber de duobus monachis*

       Fulcra tenent, at me mens bene fida Deo.
O pietas immensa Dei, fiducia quanta est
       Illis qui sperant in bonitate tua!
Abbas estiua letus cenabat in aula,
       Et fuit ex more splendida mensa uiro.
Quis melius cenare solet uel lautius illis
       Inguinis et uentris sedula cura quibus?
Lanx illata fuit, post omnia fercula tandem
       Plena medullatis ossibus ante patrem.
Torruerat dulces lento cocus igne medullas,
       Sparserat obtysim rasa piretra super.
Ossa uir exurgens dum frumine uoluit ablato,
       Gutturis obliquum crusta subintrat iter,
Deuiat in fibras esus letalis et heret,    f. 186v
       Illic pulmonis est ubi canna patens.
Tracia clausa uia est—tunc uasto ruptus hiatu—
       Non poterat pacti carceris esse memor.
Funus adhuc stabat nec molli cespite tectum,
       Cum celer emissus per mare cursor adest.
Pontificem narrat Laphitarum cede peremptum,
       Symona captiuum carceribusque datum.
Symonis iste fuit puer et mandata ferebat
       Abbati, credens quod superesset adhuc.
Depositas poscebat opes, poscebat ab illo
       Qui suus, ut uixit, fiscus et arca fuit.
Res uenit in medium. Stupet et pauet vnio fratrum.
       'Ve nobis,' clamant, 'perditus estne pater?

---

jubilant optimism may well underestimate Symon's intentions. On the other hand Symon's boy may have been sent by some other authority with the mission of restoring to the church all Symon's loot.

---

1248 Fulcra . . . at] Fultra, . . . ad **Co** | 1251 estiua] festiva **Co** | 1259 ablato] in alto **Gh**, in ablato **Ot**, ab alto **Me** | 1260 crusta] crustra **Gh**, **Co** | 1262 illic] Illuc **Me** 1263–64] om **Me** | 1268] om **Me** | 1269 fuit puer] puer fuit **Me** | 1271 poscebat . . . poscebat] poscebat . . . petebat **Me** | 1272–82] om **Me**

by his complicity in the crime. 'Let us search for the money bags. Perhaps the whole affair is a mistake and a lies. Symon is great at poisonous arts.'

The treasure chests were opened. They found two thousand drachmas (1280) and ten times tenfold myriads of gold. Here among the various ornaments of the abbot you might see rich gifts with which breasts could be decorated. Among the gems and the gold, what shone forth there was the psalter that I believe had been my mother's, for she had given it to the abbot so that he might be mild and humane and peaceful towards me. And here also there lay many well-known libels, among which mine was returned to me. Not until then did it first come into my hands, (1290) and a copy of it was made for me. For that wicked Symon had insured that I could not defend myself and hid from me the power of a defensive weapon. For he feared, not unreasonably, that the pope, or whoever might be in power now, might intervene, and he shuddered, not in vain, lest that very great Iohannes Gagetanus might do me a favour as he had before. That was the reason he had long ago removed me from the hidey-holes of his cleverness, and for seven years now he had been burning me in the fire of that conflagration.

But now Herod is dead, I am safer (1300) than the blessed Virgin Mary with her son. The urge to visit holy places pleases me and to

---

**1287** The libellus quoted above, 1147–1208. | **1296** Two members of the Gagetanus (Caitani, Gaetani) family became popes, Gelasius II (January 1118–January 1119) and Boniface VIII (1294–1303), but I suspect that the key phrase here is in l. 1294, aut quis in urbe fuit, or whoever holds the office at the moment. For the possibility

| | |
|---|---|
| 1275 | Perditus estne pater?' Nam si cum fure cucurrit, |
| | Consensu sceleris perditus esse potest. |
| | 'Queramus loculos. Res est falsaria forsan |
| | Et mentita. Uiro magnus in arte Symon.' |
| | Scrinia panduntur, auri duo millia dragmas |
| 1280 | Inueniunt decies miriadasque decem. |
| | Hic, inter uaria patris ornamenta, uideres    f. 187r [olim 186r] |
| | Dona quibus possent pectora diua capi. |
| | Interque gemmis quod ibi radiabat et auro |
| | Psalterium matris credo fuisse mee, |
| 1285 | Illud enim sibi nostra parens donarat, ut esset |
| | Mitis et humanus pacificusque michi. |
| | Hic et famosi multi iacuere libelli, |
| | Inter quos meus est redditus ille michi. |
| | Denique tunc primum manibus, michi crede, sub istis |
| 1290 | Uenit, et ipsius copia michi facta est. |
| | Cauerat infelix ne me defendere possem |
| | Abstuleratque michi Martis et ensis opem. |
| | Nam timor haut vanus foret illi ne michi papa |
| | Interpellandus aut quis in urbe foret, |
| 1295 | Horruit, haut cassum, ne maximus ille Iohannes |
| | Gagetanus opem ferret ut ante michi. |
| | Hac ratione diu me sedibus abdidit artis, |
| | Et iam septennis torruit igne rogi. |
| | At nunc Herode defuncto tutior exsto |
| 1300 | Quam pia cum puero uirgo Maria suo. |

---

that the reference might be to Pope Boniface VIII, see Introduction, p. xxiv. **1299–1300** Cf. Matth 2:19-21.

---

**1277** falsaria] fallaria **Co** | **1283 Me** adds: Quod in subripio furtive atque resummo **1284** credo] crede **Gh** | **1285–1309 Me** substitutes : Et sed et hec me temptacio tenet/Que facit instabilem ut moueam ita pedem | **1288** redditus] cognitus **Co** **1290** michi . . . est] facta michi **Co** | **1291** Cauerat] cauebat **Co** | **1294** urbe foret] orbe fuit **Gh, Co, Me** | **1295** Iohannus] uirorum **Co** | **1297** abdidit] adidit **Co** | **1299** Herode . . . exsto] defuncto sic sum michi tutus Herode **Co** | **1300** Quam] Ut **Co**

behold, great Rome, the sites of your magnificence. Perhaps there is someone there who will perceive my misfortunes in his imagination and will have some feeling of compassion. Perhaps there is someone to find a poet who will write a good poem about that guilty abbot's grave, and thus one who will say that the shepherd who scattered the sheep and tore the flock to pieces now lies under the turf. May his ashes and bones be scattered through a thousand wastelands, (1310) and let no integral part of him exist anywhere.

**Zelator:**
Neither Symon's letter nor that libel were of any worth, and they have caused anxious wrinkles on your brow. Nothing is better than a good reputation, nothing worse than those things that blacken and stain superior honours. Repute is a work of honour, repute is the quality of virtue, the crowning reward of a man, perennial glory. On earth a reputation for virtue is all that remains of us after our souls flee to the stars. I think that a good reputation is quite unwilling to remain further in this world (1320) as long as those who run monasteries stink, just as the flowers, which the cloister garden produces, have been crushed by the suspicion of the most wretched person.

For who would be so empty-headed as to believe that you would stain your devout hands with theft? There are no signs of a thief in you, but rather you bear the image of innate noble heritage. Do not marvel, however, if in the garden of religion there may grow something which deprives the delicate roses of their scent, which stains the lilies, which deprives the hyacinth of its fragrance, (1330) which neglects the balsam,

---

1301–08 Ad loca sacra . . . .diripuitque gregem]
    Nunc michi liber ego leuis et sine compede curro,
        Aera cum capto, te quoque, Roma peto.
    Spero quod hic aliquem michi sit reperire poetam,
        Qui faciat uersus ob fera busta feros.
    Uel si non carmen sacra referemus ab urbe,

Ad loca sacra michi sedet impetus ire tuosque ^(f. 187v)
    Maxima tuarum Roma uidere situs.
Forsitan est illic qui nostros mente labores
    Percipit et pectus compatientis habet.
1305  Forsitan est illic aliquem reperire poetam
    Qui faciat uersus ad rea busta bonos
Atque ita qui dicat jacet hoc sub cespite pastor
    Qui dispersit oues diripuitque gregem.
Mille per exilia cineres spargantur et ossa
1310    Ipsius et non sit pars aliquota simul.

**Zelator:**
Non bona carta fuit nec epistula Symonis ista
    Impressit tristemque tibi fronte notam.
Nil melius fama scriptis nil acrius illis
    Que fuscant titulos commaculentque probos.
1315  Fama decoris opus, uirtutis opinio fama,
    Fama corona viri, fama perhenne decus.
Hec est in terris que nobis sola remansit,
    Uirtutum postquam fugit ad astra chorus.
Arbitror in mundo simul hanc iam nolle morari
1320    Amplius, ut fetent qui loca sacra tenent,
Scilicet ut flores quos claustri germinat ortus ^(f. 188r [olim 187r])
    Aspicit infami suspicione premi.
Nam cerebri quis tam uacuus qui credere posset
    Te furto sacras commaculasse manus?
1325  Denique nulla tibi respondent signa latronis,
    Sed magis ingenui sanguinis instar habens.
Ne mirare tamen si religionis in orto
    Crescat quod teneras priuet odore rosas,
Lilia quod maculet, quod fraudet odore iacintos,

---

    Precipiat tumulo papa carere uirum.
  Mandet humo pulsum canibusque lupisque relinqui,
    Tortor ut ille ferus sit fera preda feris. **Co**
1313–14] om Me | 1315 decoris . . . uirtutis] uirtutis . . . decoris Me | 1316–26] om Me | 1326 sanguinis] numinis Co | 1327 mirare] Gh | 1329–30] om Me

which tramples the thyme. The cultivator of the church has not yet harvested his fields, nor has he divided each according to its garden bed. Now the burdock rustles bordering on the delicate violet, the harsh hemlock oppresses the fragrant thyme, wild gourds may disturb the vines, brambles the olives, ground elder the myrtle, rotting reeds the fragrant shrub. And take your case: why should you be punctured by I don't know what sorts of thorns? Not because you should perhaps have been promoted before the others. Christ knew that you were chosen. He recognised gold—(1340) and he laid on you more fire and flames. A potter testing his pots knows what will take a fierce fire or that a vat, a tile, may bear only a gentle fire.

Oh precious priest, roasted by holy flame! Oh celebrated confessor, carrying the image of a martyr. Come now, finish everything with a happy ending, stand with your feet fully grounded—refuse to give up. Even I admit that the struggle, monastic tribulation, is serious, and it is not always easy for a man to die. Christ died only once, one (1350) dutiful death was enough for him, for us innumerable deaths are more fitting. We are sinners, he is a blessed lamb on whose lips deceit is not found. Who now could suffer such bitter things worthily and completely, when he who was flawless endured so much? You do know what the insulting Jews mocked against him? 'If he is God, let him prove himself God; let him descend from the cross and break his chains.' His great hope, God, could set him free if he willed it. The ancient enemy shouts the same message in our ears, (1360) he insinuates to good men a descent from the cross. He knows that the summit of our religion lies in this, the ladder of our ascent leading to God. One can only reach the top of the

---

1341 Cf. Eccli 27:6 and Walther, *Prov* 5, no. 32921. | 1355–58 Matth 27:42, Marc 15:30-32, Luc 23:35.

---

1332 queque] quandoque **Co**, **Me** | 1333–34] om Me | 1334 olentem] aurifluum **Co** | 1336] om **Me** | 1337] add **Me** Depone propriam relinquem singula cura | 1338 eras] eris **Co** | 1341 qui] que **Me** | 1342–44] om **Me** | 1343 Ergo rogis excocte] O flammis tibi **Co** | 1344 habens] habes **Co** | 1349–50] om **Me** | 1351 sumus . . . at]

| | |
|---|---|
| 1330 | Balsama destituat, quod thimiama premat. |
| | Ecclesie cultor nondum sua messuit arua, |
| | Distinxit spacijs nec modo queque suis. |
| | Stridet adhuc lappa uiole contermina molli, |
| | Opprimit olentem seua cicuta tymum, |
| 1335 | Turbat adhuc uitem coloquintida, rampnus oliuam, |
| | Sambucus myrtum, putris arundo cyprum. |
| | Tu quoque cur tantis sis punctus nescio spinis? |
| | Ni quia pre reliquis forte probandus eras. |
| | Nouerat electum te Christus, nouerat aurum— |
| 1340 | Et tibi plus ignis addidit atque rogi. |
| | Uasa probans figulus nouit que sustinent acres   <sup style="font-size:smaller">f. 188v</sup> |
| | Queue rogos tenues tinnula testa ferat. |
| | Ergo rogis excocte sacris preciose sacerdos, |
| | Inclite confessor martiris instar habens, |
| 1345 | Nunc age, felici consummans omnia fine, |
| | Sta grauitate pedis, nec resilire uelis. |
| | Pugna quidem grauis est, fateor, claustralis agonis, |
| | Nec facile est homini tempus in omne mori. |
| | Mortuus est Christus tandem semel; vnica Christo |
| 1350 | Mors pia suffecit, nos numerosa decet. |
| | Nos peccatores sumus, agnus at ille beatus, |
| | Non fuit inuentus cuius in ore dolus. |
| | Quis digne pleneque pati modo possit amara, |
| | Cum tot pertulerit qui sine labe fuit? |
| 1355 | Scisne quid insultans Judeus risit in illum? |
| | 'Si Deus est iste, se probet esse Deum— |
| | De cruce descendat nunc et sua uincula rumpat. |
| | Liberet hunc si uult spes sua digna Deus.' |
| | Clamat idem nostris antiquus in auribus hostis, |
| 1360 | De cruce descensum suggerit ille bonis. |

---

sumus . . . et **Co**, sumus: ihud, est **Me** | 1352 fuit . . . cuius] est . . . eius **Co**, est . . . cuius **Me** | 1353 digne pleneque . . . possit] plene digneque . . . uelit **Me** | 1354 pertulerit] pertulit **Me** | 1355 Judeus] gens perfida **Ot**, gens **Me** | 1358] om **Co**, **Me** 1359 antiquus] antiquis **Gh**

walls with a ladder; no summits are accessible up steep cliffs. Before all others the cross is our closest ladder to heaven, and whoever abandons it tries in vain to approach God. Christ first bore his cross, adjusting it to the walls of heaven, and he carried that heavy burden on his shoulders. He bore the burden, he completed the job, he suffered.

And so let us bear (1370) our own share—it has a comfortable weight. The way to heaven is steep; nothing narrower than that gate; there is a secure mansion, a peaceful and quiet home. The apostle scorned Caesar's flames, the martyr scorned the fires, the confessor the chains, the virgin the threats. So why do you spend the flowering time of your life in struggle? A public cause of delight is near at hand. Let your abbot be good to you or bad, harsh or mellow, unjust or just in the character of his morals. As long as there is progress, let any old tyrant be acceptable. (1380) It does not matter under what sort of judge you become a martyr. Cain, whom the sin of treachery did not hold back, will not be justified by spilling Abel's blood.

**Persecutor:**
I am now myself again. I see, sweet brother, that a divine honeycomb drops from your lips. Your honey-like words force me to remain, for your sacred words have touched my soul. The greatest virtue has been grafted to divine words—such words usually bring sinners to justice. They are the things that lead each fugitive back to his cloister; (1390) they recover lapsed persons, they reconcile the guilty. Blessed be the advice and blessed

---

1362–66 For this interpretation of Gen 28:12 see, e.g., Alanus de Insulis, "Sermo de sancta cruce" PL 210: 223–26; Honorius Augustodunensis, "Speculum ecclesiae" PL 172: 869–72; "Scala coeli major" PL 172: 1229–40; "Scala coeli minor" PL 172: 1239–42. | **1381–82** Cf. Gen 4:9–16. | **1384–85** Cf. Cant 4:11.

Scit quod in hac culmen sit nostre religionis,
    Ascensus nostri scala propinqua Deo.
Non nisi per scalas murorum celsa petuntur,
    Abruptis gradibus culmina nulla ualent.
1365 Crux est scala polo pre cunctis proxima, quam qui
    Deserit in uanum temptat adire Deum.
Primus eam Christus celorum menibus aptans
    Intulit, atque humeris hoc graue gessit honus.
Gessit onus, compleuit opus, tulit ipse. Feramus
1370     Et nos portatum commoda pondus habet,
Ardua res celum, porta nichil arcius illa,
    Mansio secura, pace quiete domus.
Cesaris hic fasces contempnit apostolus, ignes
    Martir, confessor uincula, uirgo minas.
1375 Ergo quid in luctu consumis florida uite
    Tempora? Leticie publica causa subest.
Sit tibi prelatus malus ut bonus, asper ut unctus,
    Improbus ut morum nobilitate probus:
Dummodo proficiat, placeat quicunque tyrannus.
1380     Non refert sub quo iudice martyr eris.
Cayn nequitia quem non exercet iniqui
    Non erit effuso sanguine iustus Abel.

**Persecutor:**

Me michi iam reddi. Uideo, dulcissime frater,
    Vt tibi diuinus stillat ab ore fauus.
1385 Melleus iste tuus me cogit sermo manere,
    Strinxerunt animum nam sacra uerba meum.
Insita diuinis est uirtus maxima uerbis,
    Hec peccatores iustificare solent.
Hec sunt que claustris fugitiuos quosque reducunt,

---

1363–68] om Me | 1364 ualent] patent Ot, Co | 1369 Gessit] Gessis Co | 1370 portatum] partitum Ot, Co, Me | 1371] om Me | 1373 fasces] faces Co, falces Me | 1375 in] de Me | 1376] om Me | 1382 Me adds: Non tamen hos putes ut estimas morituros illos/Ob tui vindictam sed nouit figulus horam | 1388 solent] sollent Gh

the tongue that provided me, under your guidance, with a firm foundation.

Now my dry heart is moistened by a new dew; my first thanks goes to our profitable conversations. And I confess to you that there was one comment above all other true comments, one among many that it helps to repeat: austerity does no harm, nor does it matter under which judge or which executioner the holy victim may fall. Oh, a true proverb: Decius is worth as much as Datianus, (1400) Nero is equal to Pilate in his nature. I reckon that abbots are pulled from the dreary river Styx—just as the river is turbulent, so are their hearts. I see few that are calm, either inwardly or outwardly—I don't know what fearful rancour they harbour inside. The harsh wild gourd poisoned the prophet's pot; no domestic ingredients put such death-bearing food together. Let no one move a foot or leave either his village or his monastery in order to seek merciful abbots in new monasteries. All of them are serpents of just about a single nest, (1410) a gentler one of them will be another basilisk. Up to now I have been Cain; but now I shall fear no wounds, having been converted into a well-behaved Abel through the efficacy of the cross.

Here endeth the Book of the Two Monks

---

**1399** Both Decius and Datianus were noted for torturing Christians. For Decius see St Fabian, AASS January II, pp. 616-21, and St Lawrence, AASS, August II, pp. 485–532. For Datianus see St Vincent, AASS, January III, pp. 6–10, and SS Justus and Pastor, AASS August II, pp. 143–55. See also Prudentius, "Contra Symmachum" and "Peristefanon" in *Carmina*, ed. M.P. Cunningham, CCSL 126 (Turnhout, 1966), vol. 2, 672 and vol. 5, lines 40, 130, and 422. | **1400** For Pilatus see Matth 27:2, 11–24; Marc 15:1–15; Luc 23:1–24; Joh 18:29–40 and 19, 1-22. For Nero see Suetonius 6, 1 ff. | **1401** For the river Styx in Hades, see the note to line 274. | **1405** coloquintida, listed in Ca. instans, f. 192r, where it is said to be a type of apple (pomum) that grows near Jerusalem or as another name for a type of gourd. It is recommended as a diuretic and as a purge of phlegm and melancholy. Also effective

|      |                                                                                      |
|------|--------------------------------------------------------------------------------------|
| 1390 | Hic reparant lapsos, conciliantque reos.                                             |
|      | O quam sermo bonus quam lingua beata loquentis                                       |
|      | Que michi dat stabiles, te monitore, pedes.                                          |
|      | Iam michi rore nouo precordia sicca madescunt,                                       |
|      | Dulcibus alloquijs gratia prima redit.                                               |
| 1395 | Vnum, te fateor, super omnia uera locutum,                                           |
|      | Vnum de multis quod repetisse iuuat:                                                 |
|      | Non nocet austeritas, nec refert iudice sub quo                                      |
|      | Vel quo carnifice victima sancta cadat.                                              |
|      | O uerum eloquium, Decius ualet ut Datianus,                                          |
| 1400 | Par est Pilato condicione Nero.                                                      |
|      | E tristi prodisse reor Stigis amne patronos, <sup>f. 190r [olim 189r]</sup>          |
|      | Turbidus est amnis, turbida corda patrum.                                            |
|      | Aspicio paucos animo uel fronte serenos,                                             |
|      | Nescio quid diri fellis ab intus habent.                                             |
| 1405 | Scua prophetarum coloquintida toxicat ollam,                                         |
|      | Condit mortiferum nulla farina cibum.                                                |
|      | Nemo pedem moueat patriamque locumque relinquat,                                     |
|      | Vt querat mites per noua claustra patres.                                            |
|      | Omnes vnius sunt pene foraminis angues,                                              |
| 1410 | Mitior ex ipsis regulus alter erit.                                                  |
|      | Hinc ego iam Kayn, michi uulnera nulla timebo                                        |
|      | Factus Abel iustus sedulitate crucis.                                                |

Explicit liber de duobus monachis

---

against a tooth ache. | **1411–12** Gen 4:1-16. For commentary see Isidore of Seville, "Allegoriae quaedam scripturae sacrae" PL 83: 99; and Bede, "Hexaemeron" PL 91: 69–70.

---

**1390** Hec] Hic **Gh, Co** | **1391** O quam … loquentis] Sit benedicta dies sit felix temporis hora **Co, Me** | **1393**] om **Me** | **1395–96**] om **Me** | **1397** austeritas] affirmas **Gh, Ot** | **1399–406**] om **Me** | **1401** E tristi … patronos] Estimo prelatos flegetontis ab amne relatos **Co** | **1404** habent] habens **Co** | **1407** pedem] pedere **Gh** | **1409–10** om **Me** | **1411** uulnera] uel mala **Me** | **1413** Explicit … monachis] Explicit dyalogus metricus de religione **Me**, om **Ot, Co**

# BIBLIOGRAPHY

## Manuscripts
(Gh) Ghent, University of Ghent Library, MS 2178, ff. 155r-190r
(Gr) Graz, Universtätsbibliothek, MS 1359, ff. 2r-8r, 37r-40v
(Me) Melk, Stiftsbibliothek Melk, MS 800, ff. 55r-63r
(Co) New York City, Columbia University, Rare Book and Manuscript Library, MS X878C86/P, ff. lr-22v
Stuttgart, *Württembergischen Landesbibliothek Stuttgart, Teil 1: der ehemaligen Hofbibliothek Stuttgart* (Stuttgart, 1991) MS XIV 20.1
(Ot) Vatican City, Biblioteca Apostolica Vaticana, MS Ottoboniano lat. 522, ff. 134r-141v

## Works Consulted
Abelard, Peter, *The Story of Abelard's Adversities*, J.T. Muckle, trans. (Toronto, 1954)
*Acta Sanctorum*, eds. J. Bolandus, G. Henschenius, and J. Carnaudet, eds., 85 vols. (Paris, 1863-1931)
Alanus ab Insulis, *Anticlaudianus*, ed. R. Bossuat (Paris, 1955), "Sermo de sancta cruce" PL 210, 223-26
Augustine, *De civitate dei*, ed. Emanvel Hoffmann, CCSL 40 (Prague, Leipzig, 1899)
Beckett, Samuel, *Watt* (NY, 1959)
Bede, "Hexaemeron" PL 91
St Benedict, *Regula monasteriorum*, ed. Benno Linderbauer, Florilegium patristicum, fasc. 17 (Bonn, 1928)
Benton, John F., *Self and Society in Medieval France: The Memoires of Abbot Guibert of Nogent* (1970; reprint Toronto, 1984).
Bernard of Morval, *De contemptu mundi*, ed. H.C. Hoskier (London, 1929)
*Biblia Sacra iuxta Vulgatam Clementinam* (Rome, Tournay, Paris, 1956)
Briquet, C.M., *Les filigranes*, 2nd ed. (Leipzig, 1923)
Caesarii Heisterbacensis, *Dialogus miraculorum*, ed. Joseph Strange (Cologne, 1851)
Caesarius von Heisterbach, *Dialogus Miraculorum über die Wunder*, eds. N. Nösges and H. Schneider, Fontes Christiani (Turnhout, 2009), with German translation.
*Cambridge History of Medieval Monasticism in the Latin West*, eds. Alison J. Beach and Isabelle Cochelin, 2 vols. (Cambridge, 2020)

Cardelle de Hartmann, C., *Lateinische Dialoge 1200-1400: literaturhistorische Studie und Repertorium*, Mittellateinische Studien und Texte 37 (Leiden and Boston, 2007)

Carmody, Francis J., ed., 'Physiologus latinus versio Y,' *Classical Weekly*, 35 (1941), 95-134

Circa instans, in Yuhanna (Johannes) Serapion, *Breviarium medicinae* (f. 2r-); Serapion (Junior), *Liber de simlplici medicina* (f. 92r-); Galenus (pseudo-), *De virtute centauree* (f. 168r-); Johannes Platerarius, *Practica brevis* (f. 169r-); *Liber de simplici medicina dictus circa instans* (f. 186r-) (Venice, 1497)

Claudianus, *De raptu Proserpinae*, ed. M. Platnauer, (Loeb Classical Library, 135-36)

Conrad, L.I., Michael Neve, Vivian Nutton, Roy Porter, and Andrew Wear, *The Western Medical Tradition 800 BC to AD 1800* (Cambridge, 1995)

Crane, T.F., ed., *The Exempla of Jacques de Vitry* (repr. Liechtenstein, 1967)

Culpepper, Nicholas, *Culpepper's Complete Herbal* (reprint: Ware, Herts., 1985)

Demaitre, Luke, *Medieval Medicine: the Art of Healing from Head to Toe*, Praeger Series on the Middle Ages (Santa Barbara CA, Denver CO, and Oxford, 2013)

Derolez, Albert, T*he Paleography of Gothic Manuscript Books from the Twelfth to the Early Sixteenth Century* (Cambridge, 2002)

*Dictionnaire de theologie catholique* (Paris, 1899-1950)

Diehl, Jay, "Origen's Story: Heresy, Book Production, and Monastic Reform at Saint-Laurent de Liège," *Speculum*, 95 (2020), 1051-86

Eadmer, *The Life of St Anselm Archbishop of Canterbury*, ed. and trans. Richard Southern (Oxford, 1962)

Foucault, Michel, *Surveillir et punir* (Paris, 1975; 2nd ed. 1993)

Galteri de Castillione, *Alexandreis*, ed. Marvin L. Colker (Padua, 1978)

Goffman, Erving, *Asylums: Essays on the Social Situation of Mental Patients and Other Inmates* (London, 1987; originally published 1961)

Goltz, Dietlinde, *Mittelalterliche Pharmazie und Medizin, ... mit einem Nachdruck* [des *Antidotarium Nicolai* in] *der Druckfassung von 1471* (Stuttgart, 1976)

Gregorii magni, *Dialogi libri IV*, ed. Umberto Moricca (Rome, 1924)

Hagenmeier, Winfried, *Die datierten Handschriften der Universitätsbibliothek und anderer öffentlicher Sammlungen in Freiburg im Breisgau und Umgebung* (Stuttgart, 1989)
Harris, Carissa M., "'Yt was a woman or a womans thing': Neglected Obscene Riddles in CUL MS. Dd.5.75," *Journal of the Early Book Society*, 22 (2019), 213-23
Hervieux, L., *Les fabulistes latins*, 5 vols. (Paris, 1893-99)
Honorius Augustodunensis, "Speculum ecclesiae" PL 172, 869-72; "Scala coeli major," PL 172, 1229-40; "Scala coeli minor," PL 172, 1239-42
Horace (Q. Horatius Flaccus), *Odes and Epodes*, eds. C. E. Bennett and J.C. Rolfe (Boston, New York, Chicago, 1947)
Jezierski, Wojtek, "Verba volant, scripta manent: Limits of Speech, Power of Silence and Logic of Practice in some Monastic Conflicts of the High Middle Ages," in Steven Vanderputten, ed., *Understanding Monastic Practices of Oral Communication*, Utrecht Studies in Medieval Literacy (Turnhout, 2011), pp. 23-48
Joseph Iscanus, *Werke und Briefe*, ed. Ludwig Gompf (Leiden, 1970)
Juvenal (Decimus Iunius Iuvenalis) and Persius (Aulus Persius Flaccus) (Loeb Classical Library 91)
Isidore of Seville, "Allegoriae quaedam scripturae sacrae," PL 83, 99
Kern, Anton and Maria Mairold, *Die Handschriften der Universitätsbibliothek Graz*, vol. 1 (Leipzig, 1942; MSS 1-712), vol. II (Vienna, 1956; MSS 713-2066), vol. III (Vienna, 1967). Searchable catalogue at sosa2.uni-graz.at/sosa/katalog/index.php. (accessed 6/3/21)
Klapper, J., *Exempla aus Handschriften des Mittelalters* (Heidelberg, 1911)
A.G. Little, *Liber exemplorum ad usum praedicantium* (Aberdeen, 1908)
Migne, J.-P., *Patrologiae Cursus Completus, series latina*, 221 vols. (Paris, 1878-90)
Oliger, Livarius O.F.M., 'Bonagratia de Bergamo et eius tractatus de Christi et apostolorum paupertate,' *Archivium Franciscanum Historicum*, 22 (1929), 292-335
Ovid (P. Ovidius Naso), *Ars Amatoria* (Loeb Classical Library 232}, *Metamorphoses* Books 1-8 (LCL 42) and Books 9-15 (LCL 43), *Tristia, Ex Ponto* (LCL 151)
Petrus Alfonsi, *Disciplina clericalis*, ed. A. Hilka and W. Söderhjelm (Heidelberg, 1911)

Piccard, Gerhard, *Der Turm*, (Stuttgart, 1970), Findbuch III. Further examples at www.piccard-online.de/suche.php?sprache=dewww. (accessed 5/3/21)

Plechl, Helmut and Sophie-Charlotte Plechl, *Orbis latinus: Lexikon lateinischer geographischer Namen des Mittelalters und der Neuzeit*, 3 vols. (Braunschweig, 1972)

Pliny, (G. Plinius Secundus), *Historia naturalis*, 37 Books, 1-2 (Loeb Classical Library 330), Books 3-7 (LCL 352), Books 12-16 (LCL 370), etc.

Prudentius, "Contra Symmachum" and "Peristefanon" in *Carmina*, ed. M.P. Cunningham, CCSL 126 (Turnhout, 1966), vol. 2

Raby, F.J.E., *A History of Christian Latin Poetry*, 2nd ed. (Oxford, 1953} and *A History of Secular Latin Poetry*, 2nd ed., 2 vols. (Oxford, 1957)

Rigg, A.G., *A History of Anglo-Latin Literature 1066-1422* (Cambridge, 1992)

Samaran, Charles and Robert Marichal, *Catalogue des manuscrits en ecriture latine* (Paris, 1962)

Scarpetti, Matthias et al., *Katalog der Handschriften der Schweiz in lateinischer Schrift vom Anfang des Mittelalters bis 1550*, 3 vols. (Dietikon-Zürich, 1977-1991}

Spilling, H. (based on earlier work by W. lrtenkauf), *Die datierten Handschriften der Württembergischen Landesbibliothek Stuttgart*, Teil 1: *die datierten Handschriften der ehemaligen Hofbibliothek Stuttgart* (Stuttgart, 1991}

Statius (P. Papinius Statius), *Thebaid* books 1-7 (Loeb Classical Library 207), books 8-12 (LCL 498), *Achilleid*, ed. A. Marastoni, Bibliotheca Scriptorum Graecorum et Romanorum Teubneriana (Leipzig, 1974)

Suetonius (G. Suetonius Tranquillus), *Lives of the Caesars*, 2 vols (Loeb Classical Library 31 and 38)

Sulpicii Severi *Libri qui supersunt*, ed. Carolus Halm CSEL (Vienna, 1866) and Richard J. Goodrich, *Sulpicius Severus: the Complete Works. Introduction, Translation, and Notes* (New York, 2015)

Theodulus, *Ecloga: II canto della verita e della mensogna*, ed., Francesco Mosetti Casaretto (Florence, 1997)

Vergil (P. Vergiius Maro), *Aeneid*, Loeb Classical Library, 2 vols., *Eclogues, Georgics, Aeneid* Books 1-6 (LCL 63) and *Aeneid books 7-12* (LCL 64)

Waddell, Helen, *The Desert Fathers* (London: Constable, 1936; frequently reprinted)

Walter of Châtillon, *The Shorter Poems*, ed. and trans. D.A. Traill, Oxford Medieval Texts (Oxford, 2013)
Walther, Hans, *Das Streitgedicht in die lateinischen Literatur des Mittelalters* (Munich, 1920)
Walther, Hans, *Proverbia sententiaeque latinitatis medii aevi*, Carmina Medii Aevi Posterioris Latina, 5 vols. (Göttingen, 1963-67)
Walther, Hans, *Initia carminum ac versuum medii aevi posterioris latinorum* (Göttingen, 1959)
Werner, Jakob, *Lateinische Sprichwörter und Sinnsprüche des Mittelalters* (Heidelberg, 1912)
William of Ockham, *Dialogus*, eds. J. Kilcullen et al. (London, 1995-2015)
Witter, Martin and François Masai, *Manuscrits datés conservés en Belgique*, vol. 1: 819-1400 (Brussels, 1968)
Wölfel, Hans, *Das Arzneidrogenbuch Circa instans* ... (Berlin, 1939)
*Ysengrimus*, ed. Ernst Voigt, (Halle, 1884) and more recently ed. Jill Mann (Cambridge MA, 2013) with English translation

www.ingramcontent.com/pod-product-compliance
Lightning Source LLC
Chambersburg PA
CBHW020419230426
43663CB00007BA/1231